D0065784

[reclaim!]

[reclaim!]

A Practical Guide *to* Restoring Wholeness

matthew kelly

with jack beers

BLUE SPARROW
North Palm Beach, Florida

BLUE
sparrow

Copyright © 2021
Kakadu, LLC
Published by Blue Sparrow

ISBN: 978-1-63582-246-5 (hardcover)

Cover Layout and Interior by Ashley Dias

10   9   8   7   6   5   4   3   2   1

FIRST EDITION

Printed in the United States of America

> "The life that wants to live in you
> is different than the life you are living."
>
> *Matthew Kelly*

[table of contents]

[prelude]

Each year for as long as I can remember, Matthew selects a word to walk and talk with him throughout the year. In the past, he's selected words like *simplify, believe, surrender, gratitude, wonder,* and many others. This year his word is [*reclaim*].

Last week, Matthew and I spent about three hours together discussing what that word means to him.

For our conversation, Matthew was in his home office. I say "office," but honestly it feels more like a small art gallery than an office when you first walk in. There are paintings hung 360 degrees throughout the entire room. Each time I'm there, I secretly hope Matthew will excuse himself for a few minutes so I have a chance to get lost in the possibilities of just one of the paintings before me.

As you might expect, just to the right of his desk is a giant bookshelf. Matthew owns over 6,000 books but there are only about 100 or so packed like sardines in his office. The bookcase contains some classics but also some titles I've never heard of before. There is something about a book worthy of a spot in Matthew's top 100 that gives it the sense of a must-read.

To the left of his desk is an old architecture's chest with an endless number of drawers. When I say "endless" you may be tempted to think that means about 30 or 40. But that's not even close. When I say endless, I mean hundreds. Seriously, I doubt I can even count high enough to arrive at a final number of drawers in this chest.

If you want to see a wry smile inch up the side of Matthew's face, just ask him about this chest. You'll discover it's where he houses more than 400 of his book ideas. Each idea has its own drawer and each one is somewhere along a spectrum that ranges from a title with a few scribbled notes to several full drafts. The drawers being just an inch and a half thick, make them perfect for holding a manuscript.

Most people never write a book in an entire lifetime. Even most of the people who set out to write a book, never finish it. Yet here is the author of over 30 books just itching to get after the next idea on his mind and in his heart.

I've been working with Matthew for nearly seven years now and whenever I get the chance to sit down with him in a casual setting like this one, I'm excited for two reasons. The first is the hope that one of his five children would decide to wander in unexpectedly. The last time this happened, Matthew's youngest had escaped bath time. He burst into the room to the sound of his siblings cheering him on. He was covered in soap suds hoping to find refuge in his father's arms from the dread of bath time. You never find Matthew happier than when he's with one of his children.

The second reason is that Matthew is the most

interesting man I know. In all the time we've spent together, I don't think I've ever brought up a topic he hasn't spent hours and hours thinking about. More well-read and more well-traveled than anyone I know, Matthew has more insights into the human condition than he has drawers for book ideas. After an afternoon together, I find myself chewing on something he said for days and days. These conversations have literally changed the course of my life.

This conversation felt different though. The stakes seemed higher. I felt a responsibility to you, the reader. I went into the conversation knowing I stood in your place, questioning and prodding Matthew on what it means to [reclaim] such critical areas of life as: enthusiasm, dissatisfaction and contentment, guarding your heart, emotional boundaries, love of learning, our souls in a secular world, priorities, money and things, and hope for the future.

This book is the fruit of our time together. The

majority of it is our actual conversation. You will find both my questions and his answers on each topic placed between an inspirational story and a short article on five ways you can integrate Matthew's insights into your daily life.

We've never produced a book quite like this. It's a side of Matthew we've never shared before.

For the last decade or so, Matthew has been more and more willing to reveal his own struggle to live the message he's been sharing for the last 30 years. I think it's made his work more effective and that quality is on full display within these pages. As you read, you will meet Matthew as a friend talking to another friend about life, its challenges, and its opportunities. It's his unpolished thoughts and in-the-moment comments on things he too is wrestling that make this book special.

Before I pass it on to Matthew to introduce the book, I wanted to share with you a few notes I took during the conversation. There are many aspects of my work that I consider a privilege. The mission itself stands alone as the greatest privilege of all. But the coolest one has to be sitting across the table from Matthew talking through a draft of his latest book.

Usually Matthew will gather a small group of trusted advisors, ask us a question, and then sit back and listen as we rigorously and passionately debate what's working, what needs improvement, and most controversial of all... what should get cut before publishing the book.

Over the years, some incredible content has been cut. It's always for the best but it is never done without breaking at least one heart. This time around, there were five insights from Matthew that didn't fit within the context of a particular chapter but nonetheless were too strong to remain on the cutting room floor. I believe they are critical to extracting the most you can from the book:

1. To [reclaim] something is to return to its rightful place something that has gone missing or to

enter into a right relationship with something been distorted.

2. Some things *cannot* be [reclaimed]. But that isn't a cause for losing hope. There are always things that *can* be [reclaimed] that facilitate healing and give us the strength and courage to move on and step into the next phase or experience in our life.

3. When I look back on things that I've lost, it's important to remember to be kind to myself and know that sometimes I didn't get a voice or didn't have the strength to prevent whatever it was from being taken away from me.

4. It's not possible to [reclaim] something by accident. It's something that I have to go out and intentionally [reclaim]. I can't stumble on it and it cannot happen on its own.

5. Most things that are worth doing require courage. [Reclaiming] something that has been lost is no different. It requires great courage. Whenever that feels daunting, it's important

to remember that God wants me to be in right relationship with his creation. He will give me whatever I need for that to happen, including the courage to do that which I am otherwise too afraid to do.

I hope this book is the start of something meaningful in your life. I hope the wisdom contained within its pages can help you in some small way improve your relationships, your health, your career, your spirituality, or some other area of your life. And I hope you accept the invitation to [reclaim] the parts of yourself that allow you to experience the wholeness God made you for.

Jack Beers
August, 2021

[introduction]

When people share with me what is happening deep in their souls, they often say things like...

"I feel like something is missing."

"I feel like there must be more to life."

"I feel like I have so much more to offer."

People younger than you would think, and people older than you would expect, share these very same sentiments.

We describe them as feelings, but they are not. Well, they may be feelings, but they are also so much more than that. We describe them as feelings because we lack two things: the courage to claim them as sacred truths and the spiritual language to adequately describe them.

Worse than lacking the courage to claim these as sacred truths about ourselves, we often treat them as human malfunctions. We think of them as negative experiences. We view them as problems to be solved. We think that something is wrong with us, and that we need to be fixed.

Nothing could be further from the truth. When you experience this type of yearning and restlessness, you don't need to be fixed, and you are not malfunctioning. When you sense that something is missing, that there must be more to life, or that you have so much more to offer—something is very, very right!

The message you are receiving is from the very deepest part of you. The most authentic part of you is trying to get your attention. You are being beckoned by the truest part of you, the part of yourself that is simply incapable of betraying itself, and outright refuses to settle for anything less than the-very-best-version-of you.

Your soul is trying to get your attention, and ignoring the soul never ends well.

Listen. Follow. Go where it leads you. Don't

brush these messages aside. Don't try to avoid them or pretend they don't exist. Be patient. After all, if you cannot be patient with your very self, how will you ever muster the character to be patient with life as it unfolds and with other people?

Another mistake we make is to get frustrated thinking we have already dealt with these matters. These are not once-in-a-lifetime phenomenon. They tend to emerge anew whenever necessary, in different seasons of life, especially during transitions.

And we are constantly experiencing the transitions of life, though we often don't acknowledge them. We transition from life in the womb to life outside the womb, and so it begins. That first transition is traumatic for an infant, and many of life's transitions after are also traumatic. And unacknowledged trauma is the hardest trauma to make peace with.

We transition from high school to college, from college to the workplace, from one job to another, from one romantic relationship to another, from being a child to being a parent, from being healthy to dealing with illness, from a bustling home with children to an empty nest, from being parents to being grandparents, to name but a sampling of life's transitions.

Life is full of transitions. Life is a transition.

So, if you have the sense that something is missing, you are absolutely and 100% right. Don't doubt that. Explore it. Resist the temptation to be in a hurry to resolve it and accept its invitation to journey wherever it leads you.

Toward the end of each year, I spend time reflecting on the year that has been and the year that is to come. As part of one of the exercises that make up this annual ritual, I choose a word to serve as a theme for the coming year. The word I chose for this year was [*reclaim!*].

Life is a series of gains and losses. Those gains and losses take many forms. Friends come and go, opportunities come and go, and we gift little pieces of ourselves to the special people in our lives while other people steal pieces. Sometimes logical, sometimes paradoxical. We gain things we wish we could lose, and lose things we spend the rest of our lives mourning or trying to recover.

Reclaim is defined as: to retrieve, recover, or obtain the return of something previously lost, given, or stolen.

It's a good definition, but I'd like to add one small, but important, amendment to it. To reclaim something is to retrieve, recover, or obtain a *right relationship* with something previously lost, given or stolen.

What do you need to reclaim?

It's time to reclaim whatever has been lost, stolen, or given in error (either because we deceived ourselves or were manipulated by others). It's time to reclaim your life. It's time to reclaim yourself.

There are so many ways we need to reclaim. In preparing to write this book, I began by brainstorming a list with some colleagues and we quickly arrived at more than 100 aspects of life and self that needed to be reclaimed.

I include that list here, not as a definitive list, but to help you brainstorm your own list: Dreams, Energy, Creativity, Peace of Mind, Spirituality, Hope for the Future, Time, Personal Finances, Friendships, Fortitude, Stillness, Family, Love of Reading, Psychological Safety, Soul, Heart, Environments, Financial Freedom, Marriage, Kindness, Health, Body, Love of Learning, Mental Health, Meaning of Life, Childlike Wonder, Independence, Stuff, Intimacy, Goodness, Needs, Senses, Inspiration, Attitude, Peace, Confidence, Responsibilities, Relationship with Money, Family, Integrity, Ability to Say No, Space, Curiosity, Freedom, Silence, Wonder, To Do List, Relationship with Things, Privacy, Gratitude, Purpose, Ideas, Past, Present, and Future, Solitude, Fragility, Priorities, Relationship with Money and Things, Boundaries, Hope, Wellbeing, Content Diet, Trust, Dependence, Vulnerability,

Career, Respect, Patience, Comfort, Present Moment Awareness, Vocation, Openness, Humility, Vision, Appreciation, Relationship to Truth, Beauty, and Goodness, Voice, Habits, Courage, Decisions, Judgement Choices, Faith, Sense of Adventure, Love, Decisivencss, Social Life, Joy, Flexibility, and Contentment.

I have not written about all of these in detail in this small volume, but I do believe the ideas and principles you will find here will serve you regardless of what aspects of yourself and your life you are being beckoned to reclaim. Unlike other books I've written in the past, this one contains a varicty of different types of content. You never know when the right phrase, the right idea, the right question, the right word is going to be exactly what you needed at exactly the right time.

As we set off on this journey together, I invite you to consider the other option. Reclaim... or what? What is the other option? If you don't reclaim what you uniquely need to reclaim, what will happen? What won't happen? What damage will be done to the best and purest parts of you?

If we reclaim what is rightfully ours and help others to do the same, I believe we will enter a new period of human flourishing. This is my hope, dream, and prayer for you: May you flourish as the person God created you to be—unique and wonderful—like never before.

So, if you have the sense that something is missing, or that there must be more to life, or that you have so much more to contribute... I am incredibly excited for you. Don't ignore it, avoid it, or push it away. Embrace it as a precious gift. If you do, I promise you, something wonderful is about to happen!

Matthew Kelly

[enthusiasm]

intense and eager enjoyment, interest, or approval

[a bit of inspiration]

"It is not the critic who counts; not the man who points out how the strong man stumbles, or where the doer of deeds could have done them better. The credit belongs to the man who is actually in the arena, whose face is marred by dust and sweat and blood; who strives valiantly; who errs, who comes short again and again, because there is no effort without error and shortcoming; but who does actually strive to do the deeds; who knows great enthusiasms, the great devotions; who spends himself in a worthy cause; who at the best knows in the end the triumph of high achievement, and who at the worst, if he fails, at least fails while daring greatly, so that his place shall never be with those cold and timid

souls who neither know victory nor defeat."
- Theodore Roosevelt

[Q & A with Matthew]

[**Jack**]: Let's jump into our first topic. I think with all of these topics it's important to get clear on a definition of what we are talking about. And I think enthusiasm is one of the most important to define.

How would you define enthusiasm? What is it and what does it look like?

[**Matthew**]: I've spent a lot of time on this one outside of this project over the last couple of years. If I had to tell you what enthusiasm is in one sentence, I really believe that enthusiasm is the secret to eternal youth.

I stumbled onto this while working on Dynamic Catholic's upcoming Catholic Moment project on aging and dying. I was looking at elderly people and I realized: okay we've got this person here, still very engaged in life, and this person here seemingly going through the motions. And they represent enormous groups within the elderly demographic.

What's the difference? Essentially what I arrived at was enthusiasm.

It might be an oversimplification, but everything good in life adds to our store of enthusiasm and everything bad in life takes from that store of enthusiasm.

And I mean everything. A good parent adds to that store of enthusiasm and a bad parent drains it. Not that it's binary, but an unintentional or selfish parent takes from that store of enthusiasm. We all know parents who have psychologically or emotionally beaten the enthusiasm out of their children before they were 5 or 10 or 15 or 21..

I really do believe that enthusiasm is the secret to the fountain of youth. Enthusiasm is the secret to staying young in ways that matter and are possible. But it is also the secret to aging gracefully, which is an art unto itself that nobody teaches, or even talks about.

"It's faith in something and enthusiasm for something that makes a life worth living."
- *Oliver Wendell Holmes*

[**Jack**]: That makes me think about how there are certain seasons of life in which enthusiasm is celebrated and other seasons of life when enthusiasm is considered unattractive.

Like enthusiasm in a child is one of the most attractive things. It naturally sparks enthusiasm in other people.

But, in the work that I've done with teens—13, 14, and 15 years old—I've seen that once you get to about that age, enthusiasm is basically outlawed.

It's like you get to a certain point in adulthood and it's inappropriate to be excited about life and excited about doing things.

And then, enthusiasm comes back into style again. There are few things more attractive than an old person who is constantly smiling.

Do you think it's true that enthusiasm comes in and out of style through the seasons of life? And why do you think the culture goes through these periods of trying to temper people's enthusiasm?

[**Matthew**]: Yeah, so I do think that's true, though I think the culprit or the villain is different at different times.

For example, in the teen years I think it is sort of a cocktail of peer pressure and insecurity, which is natural at that age. It has a rightful place, because a person is trying to develop a sense of self. When we're trying to develop a sense of self, we are naturally insecure and rightfully so. But combine that with peer pressure and I think you can end up killing enthusiasm. So, it's important to say the malfunction is peer pressure. I don't think the malfunction is necessarily the larger society or culture for teenagers.

I have also seen grown adults mock other grown adults for being too enthusiastic about a project at work or something happening in their lives. This mocking of enthusiasm is especially unattractive, even repulsive.

[**Jack**]: So clearly, there are a lot of potential misconceptions around enthusiasm.

Are there any other misconceptions on enthusiasm that you want to address?

[**Matthew**]: Well, you gave the example of people who are always happy or constantly smiling. It's the "constantly" that gives enthusiasm a bad reputation.

The person who is always joyful cannot be trusted. Because there is something disingenuous about always being joyful. That's not life. We all experience pain and suffering, disappointment, and betrayal. Life is messy. Everyone's got something going on and so the person who is always smiling, I think there's something disingenuous about that. It's a persona of types.

First and foremost, we are called to be enthusiastically ourselves. There is room for happiness, sadness, and every other emotion and experience in that.

[**Jack**]: Alright, let's talk about the relationship between enthusiasm and circumstances. For a long time, I assumed that enthusiasm was something that was facilitated through exciting things happening in life, that it was the result of circumstances.

Can you be enthusiastic regardless of circumstances or does enthusiasm have to be dependent on circumstance?

[**Matthew**]: No, it doesn't. I think it's important to point out that the goal is not to be enthusiastic all the time. I don't have to be enthusiastic about going to the dentist. I just don't, and so again, these principles don't have to be universally applied.

But we also can't wait around hoping that the right circumstances for enthusiasm will strike. We must learn to stoke the flames of enthusiasm in our lives. There will be times when enthusiasm rightfully belongs, and we don't naturally have it— it didn't show up on that day. It's crucial that we learn how to stoke and fan the flames of enthusiasm, so we can get it to grow.

It is also important that we learn to recognize when our enthusiasm is waning and what is causing that.

There are going to be circumstances that rob us

of our enthusiasm. But it is not like you have one tank of enthusiasm for your life and when it's empty, you're done. I feel like a lot of people live their life that way, saying: "I used to have that kind of enthusiasm." What they are really saying is, "I already used up all my enthusiasm and don't have any left." But that just isn't true. Our enthusiasm tank can be refilled, and we can do things to refill it, and we can do things to refill other people's enthusiasm.

Depending on how you see life, circumstances good and bad take on massively different meanings. I think the more spiritual we become, and the more we understand life as a quest to become the best-version-of-ourselves, the more we realize that truth about circumstances.

St. Ignatius wrote about indifference as a spiritual quality, as a way of surrendering to God's will. It's the idea that you shouldn't prefer health to illness or prefer riches to poverty. He's got a whole list. It's an extreme form of detachment. But it's something I have always struggled with because part of me feels like God does actually prefer health to sickness. And yet, I accept that both are opportunities to grow, and that the downside might be a better opportunity to grow. These difficult situations force us to grow, and human beings don't naturally seek out growth.

"We must make ourselves indifferent to all created things, as far as we are allowed... Consequently...we should not prefer health to sickness, riches to poverty, honor to dishonor, a long life to a short life. The same holds for all other things. Our one desire and choice should be what is more conducive to the end for which we were created."
(#23 of The Spiritual Exercises of Saint Ignatius of Loyola)

[**Jack**]: Yeah, it's an interesting point because I'm not a product of my circumstances, or at least I try to live like I'm not a product of my circumstances. But I also have to respond to my circumstances appropriately.

For instance, if my grandmother dies, my emotions are a product of the circumstance, because they should be in many ways. I should feel sad that day. And I should appear sad, I shouldn't be doing cartwheels that day.

[**Matthew**]: Okay, so there's some very complex statements there. We don't choose our emotions. So, I don't think it's accurate to say you should feel sad that day.

I do agree with what you followed that up with, which is that you should behave in a somber and respectful way, regardless of what you're feeling, because many people are dealing with a grieving process.

But I think it's possible your grandma could die,

and a lot of people could go into a numb state. They don't feel sad or know how to deal with it, and then three weeks later it's like boom, it just demolishes them, and all of a sudden, they're crawled up in a ball on the floor weeping and they don't know how it happened.

Grief has a different timetable for different people.

[**Jack**]: So how do you stoke the flames of enthusiasm?

[**Matthew**]: I think that ties into what people mistakenly believe about enthusiasm and the first thing is, in order to stoke the flame of enthusiasm you actually have to believe that you have some influence over it. It is not just a wind that you have no control over, that comes when it wants and leaves when it wants. You have influence.

There are classical ways of stoking enthusiasm. Doing things that you were very enthusiastic about as a child tends to be one of those things that stokes enthusiasm and helps us develop a sense of rootedness and excitement for life. Even if you don't really feel like doing those things that you did as a child, there's something about doing them that gets you back in touch with that raw enthusiasm of childhood.

But then, I think the question is really a function of self-awareness. Enthusiasm does rise up in you. Just like you can sense hunger, thirst, tiredness, or lust rise up in you, you can sense enthusiasm too. So, pay attention to when enthusiasm rises up in you. What causes that? Who causes that? Maybe it's reading or maybe it's taking some time in nature. Maybe it's spending time with kids or journaling. It could be different things for everyone.

Everyone needs to know what stokes enthusiasm for them and I can't tell you what it should be for you. I can't say "hey it's *this* for everyone," or "hey, for you, it's definitely *this* thing." Some of life's work can only be done by us. And we're the only ones who get the soul-deep information necessary to come to the conclusion.

I don't feel when enthusiasm flames up in you, you're the only person who feels that. People close to you may be able to tell by the way you hold yourself, by the way your eyes animate and things like that, but it is deeply personal work.

All that being said, I do believe that as human beings we are relational. We are created to be in relationship with each other. But we encounter so many people and every person is at a different place in their journey. So, being around some will fill you with enthusiasm and being around others will not. It's important to be aware of that, and to take note. Who are the people who fill you with enthusiasm?

I'll say one more thing that may sound strange at first. My own quest for enthusiasm has led me to have many dead friends. The great souls of every age have never been more accessible to us as guides, friends, coaches, mentors, and teachers. I am of course a lover of books, but I am constantly amazed that for twenty dollars you can have access to the great minds of any age on any topic. They will come and sit with you in the big comfy chair where you like to read and share their hearts, minds, and souls with you. I find that to be outrageously wonderful. And I draw much of my enthusiasm from the great men and women of history.

"Flaming enthusiasm, backed up by horse sense and persistence, is the quality that most frequently makes for success."
- Dale Carnegie

[**Jack**]: In the past, you've said that "Energy is our most valuable resource."

How is enthusiasm related to energy?

[**Matthew**]: To put the energy quote in context, I wrote that in the 1990s. And it was written toward the end of the 90s, when our culture was coming out of an almost 20-year obsession with time management. My observation was that time management was important, and still is today. But by the end of the 90s, I also considered it a prerequisite, simply permission to play. It was no longer the competitive advantage it had been touted as.

If you want to participate at a high level in anything, you need to be able to manage your time effectively. Maybe in the late 70s and early 80s it was a competitive advantage because that science had not developed. But as that science developed, more and more people mastered time management, and it was no longer a competitive advantage. It just became an expected part of the new playing field.

And so, I was asking: Where does the next competitive advantage come from in human development? This question led me to conclude that energy management was the key to the next level.

We all get 24 hours each day. Nobody gets more. It is one of the most democratic aspects of the human experience. You only get 24 hours and there is something finite about that. You can be exceptional at managing your time, but there is also something finite about that. But our energy is almost infinite and holds much greater possibilities. I watch my children and often think to myself, "If I had that kind of energy, I could change the world."

So, the connection between energy and enthusiasm is clear. You've never seen an enthusiastic person who was lazy, tired, burnt out, or exhausted. These things don't go together, right? Enthusiasm requires a certain amount of energy, and so, if you're running on empty from an energy point of view, it doesn't matter if you try to fan the flame of enthusiasm, those embers stay pretty cold.

Our experience of life expands or contracts according to how much energy we have. Increase your energy in any of the many ways that is possible, and you will increase your capacity for life. Think about that. Five words: Your capacity to experience life. That is no small thing.

"Enthusiasm is the electricity of life. How do you get it? You act enthusiastic until you make it a habit."

- Gordon Parks

[Five Ways to Invite More Enthusiasm into Your Life]

When was the last time you felt amazing? Trauma, sickness, anxiety, depression, loss—so many things threaten to rob us of enthusiasm in life. And after difficult seasons in our lives, it is natural to wonder if we will ever feel amazing again. Is it even possible? It is possible, but our wounded hearts are understandably tentative. If your heart is tentative, or if you've lost your passion for life, here are five concrete things you can do to infuse your daily life with enthusiasm.

1. **Prioritize your legitimate needs.**

   Listening and responding to your legitimate needs is a prerequisite for living enthusiastically. Poor sleep, diet, and exercise habits lower your capacity for enthusiasm exponentially. Take a walk today, make yourself a healthy meal, get at least 7 hours of sleep tonight... and watch your enthusiasm begin to grow!

2. **Schedule 15 minutes every day to do something you love doing.**

   Have you ever wondered why children are so consistently enthusiastic? Many reasons, but one of the most important is that they do so many things every day just for the joy of it. You don't have to spend all day, or all week, doing something you love, schedule fifteen minutes a day this week to paint, write, fix up an old car, or whatever it is you are most passionate about at this time in your life. It will bring a new level of enthusiasm to your daily life.

3. **Say 'no' to those people and things that drain you.**

Who is the most enthusiastic person you know? If you think about it, you will likely realize that the most enthusiastic people in your life are the people who aren't afraid to say 'no' to the people and activities that drain them of energy and life. Develop an awareness of who and what drains your enthusiasm. Protect your enthusiasm by learning to say 'no.'

4. **Spend time with enthusiastic people.**

The people we surround ourselves with either raise or lower our standards. They either help us to become the-best-version-of-ourselves or encourage us to become a lesser version of ourselves. We become like our friends. Your enthusiasm is probably the average of the five people you spend the most time with. If you wish to raise your level of enthusiasm in life, surround yourself with enthusiastic people.

5. **Dream.**

Dreams animate us. They literally breathe new life into us. And what dreams do for individuals, they also do for relationships, teams, organizations, and communities. The pursuit of dreams creates passion, energy, enthusiasm, and vitality. When we are in touch with our dreams, we consistently believe that the future can be bigger and/or better than the past.

It's time for you to flourish. It's time to dance with life again.

You can't do it alone. You need an environment that is uniquely supportive. That includes people, food, sleep, exercise, prayer, and reflection, feeding your mind with healthy ideas, and ridding your environment of toxicity. And don't forget: Everyone who really cares about you wants you to flourish.

When was the last time you felt amazing? It's

time for your answer to this question to enter the present tense again.

The life that wants to live in you is different than the life you are living.

[dissatisfaction & contentment]

a particular feeling of displeasure or disappointment;
a state of happiness and satisfaction

[a bit of inspiration]

Once upon a time there was an investment banker. He lived in New York City, was phenomenally successful, and made a ton of money. But his life was busy, noisy, and very stressful.

So, once a year, he would leave the city and go down to a small coastal village in Mexico. For two weeks he would rest, relax, and allow himself to be rejuvenated.

One day he was standing on the pier just before lunch, looking out to sea, when he noticed a small fishing boat coming into dock. He thought this was a little strange, because most of the fishermen used to stay out late into the afternoon so they could catch as many fish as possible, before coming in and preparing the fish for market.

Curiosity overcame him. So, he walked over to where the fishing boat was about to dock. Looking into the boat, he saw just one fisherman and several large yellowfin tuna.

"How long did it take you to catch those fish?" he said to the fisherman.

"Not very long," the fisherman replied with a smile.

"Is there something wrong with your boat?" the American asked.

"Oh, no," the fisherman said. "In thirteen years, I have never had a problem with the boat."

The American was a little perplexed, so he asked the fisherman, "Why don't you stay out there longer and catch more fish?"

The fisherman smiled again and said, "I have plenty for my family's immediate needs. Some of the fish we can eat, and others we can sell or trade for the other things we need."

"But it's not even lunchtime. What do you do with the rest of your time?"

"In the morning," the fisherman explained, "I like to sleep late. When I wake, I fish a little, mostly just for the pleasure of fishing. In the afternoon I play with my children and take siesta with my wife. In the evenings I have dinner with my family. And then, when my children are sleeping, I stroll into the village, where I sip wine and play guitar with my amigos."

The American scoffed and said, "I'm a Harvard MBA and I can help you."

The fisherman was a little skeptical, but nonetheless he obliged and asked, "How?"

"You should fish longer every day," the American counseled, "late into the afternoon. This way you will catch more fish, make more money, and you can buy a bigger boat. With the bigger boat you will catch even more fish, make even more money, and then you can buy another boat and hire another man to work the second boat."

"But what then?" the fisherman inquired.

"Oh, we are just getting started," the American volleyed. "With two boats you'll catch even more fish and make even more money, and before you know it, you'll have a whole fleet of boats and every man in the village looking for work will come to you."

"But what then?" the fisherman asked.

"Before too long, you can cut out the middleman, sell your fish direct to the cannery, and make more money. As your fleet of boats continues to expand, you can build your own cannery. And before you know it, you'll be able to leave this small coastal village, move to Mexico City, and manage your expanding enterprise."

"But what then?" the fisherman persisted.

"Well then, you can begin to ship your fish to different parts of the world. Down into Asia and Australia and up into North America. And as demand grows for your fish, you can leave Mexico City, move to Los Angeles, open a distribution plant there, and begin to ship your fish to Europe and every corner of the globe."

"But what then?" the fisherman asked again.

The American continued, "By then your business

will be one of the greatest ventures of the industry. You can move to New York City and manage your empire from the epicenter of the business world."

"How long will all this take?" The fisherman asked.

"Twenty-five, maybe thirty years," the banker explained.

"But what will I do then?" the fisherman asked.

The American's eyes lit up like a Christmas tree. "That's the best part," he said. "When the time is just right, you can go down to Wall Street, list your business as a public company, offer an IPO, and make millions and millions of dollars."

"Millions?" the fisherman asked.

"More money than you ever dreamed you could earn in ten lifetimes," the American explained.

"But what then?" the fisherman asked.

The American didn't know what to say. He had reached his climax. He was stumped. But then a thought crossed his mind and triggered an idea, and he turned once more to the fisherman and spoke.

"Well then, you could move to a small coastal

village... you could sleep late... You could fish just for
the pleasure of fishing... In the afternoons you could
take siesta with your wife... In the evenings you could
have dinner with your family... and then you could
stroll into the village and sip wine and play guitar with
your amigos..."

[Q & A with Matthew]

[**Jack**]: Let's talk about dissatisfaction and contentment, which you've paired together.

Did you pair dissatisfaction and contentment
together because they're opposites or did you
have another reason?

[**Matthew**]: I paired them because they both have
a rightful place in our lives. Both dissatisfaction
and contentment are very powerful servants, and
they are both companions for the journey.

For example, are we called to become a-better-version-of-ourselves each day? Yeah, we are. Are we called to be content with what God has done in us today? If we really strive to improve ourselves in a day, week, month, or year, we are called to be content with what God has done in us in that day, week, month, or year. But not to the extent that contentment turns into a reason, excuse, or justification not to wake up tomorrow morning and get back at it.

Maybe it's good to wake up in the morning dissatisfied and good to go to bed at night content. Maybe that's the balance.

Pope John XXIII had a prayer he prayed like a child at the end of each day. "God, I've done the best I could in your service today. I'm going to bed. It's your church. Take care of it!"

I've always loved that prayer. It demonstrates the natural tension between the desire to improve, dissatisfaction, and contentment—and at the end of the day it rightfully places all these things in the heart of God. This is what it means to be in right relationship with anything. Knowing when to hold on, when to let go, and whose arms to place things in when we let go.

"Paradoxically, I have found peace because I have always been dissatisfied. My moments of depression and despair turn out to be renewals, new beginnings. If I were once to settle down and be satisfied with the surface of life, with its divisions and its cliches, it would be time to call in the undertaker... So, then, this dissatisfaction which sometimes used to worry me and has certainly, I know, worried others, has helped me in fact to move freely and even gaily with the stream of life."

- Thomas Merton

[**Jack**]: That's a really interesting way to look at the relationship between the two.

How do you think contentment and dissatisfaction are currently viewed in society?

[**Matthew**]: I believe that many view contentment as a weakness. Contentment is seen as you quit, you settled. I don't think that people believe that you can be content and still be in the race, or in the quest, or in the game, or whatever aspect of life is being discussed. But I think there is great wisdom in tapping into our dissatisfaction and I think there is great wisdom in being able to be content.

The life that wants to live in you is different than the life you are living. As we go through each of these topics this is a singular truth that binds them all together. But I think it's particularly true when it comes to dissatisfaction and contentment. Because the life that wants to live in you is the life of God. He wants to animate you with his life. And it is different from the life that you are living.

You're living the life you're living because of the life that you're allowing to live in you. Or possibly because of the life you're preventing from living in you, which of course we do every day in degrees. What I am trying to say is that there are times when we invite God to live in us completely, times when we ignore or try to block his presence within us, and times when we're on the fence.

Contentment and dissatisfaction are inner qualities. They are deeply personal and intricately personalized. What brings one person contentment will leave another in the depths of dissatisfaction, because we are each called to live lives according to the gifts and personality God has uniquely endowed us with.

When we are dissatisfied with life, we are usually focused on doing and having. Contentment comes from becoming. Accomplishments, worldly possessions, and money don't lead to contentment.

Quite the opposite in fact. They tend to increase our appetite for more of the same. It's like drinking a drink that makes you thirsty. There's no lasting contentment in the things of this world.

Contentment is holy and it is an inner quality, and it comes from allowing the life that wants to live in us to consume us.

[**Jack**]: As you were talking, it made me think of the movie *Ford vs Ferrari*. I think it's a great film. There is a line in it that I was looking at today:

"When I was 10 years old, Pop said to me, 'Son, it's a truly lucky man who knows what he wants to do in this world 'cause that man will never work a day in his life.' But there are a few, a precious few—and hell, I don't know if they're lucky or not—but there are a few people who find something they have to do. Something obsesses them. Something that if they can't do it, it's going to drive them clean out of their mind."

[**Matthew**]: That is a fantastic and brilliant. I think they are the lucky ones. And I think we spend far too little time, effort, and energy as a society helping young people discover themselves enough to find that one thing that they are uniquely suited to, most suited to.

What I love about the quote is that it captures both dissatisfaction and contentment. Because even while you're obsessing, even while you're pursuing your dissatisfaction, you can be profoundly content that you are one of the ones that has found what to do with your life.

[**Jack**]: Yeah I was thinking about it and wondering, *is dissatisfaction a prerequisite to doing something great?*

[**Matthew**]: Yes. I think it is. Obsession is an expression of dissatisfaction in many ways. Einstein, Newton, Edison, Alexander Graham Bell, Benjamin

Franklin, Henry Ford, Stephanie Kwolek, Mary Anderson, Hedy Lamarr, Tesla, and Orville and Wilbur Wright were all people driven by a profound dissatisfaction with how things were and were visionaries who saw what was possible. Were they ever able to enjoy what they accomplished? Were they able to enter into periods of contentment? I don't know.

So, to answer your question directly. Yes, I believe dissatisfaction is a prerequisite for doing something great. But I also believe that you can accomplish great things driven by dissatisfaction and still experience an other-worldly contentment. We see this on full display in Francis of Assisi.

[**Jack**]: Another thing I have been thinking about is the relationship between contentment and the attachments we have in life.

What role do material objects have on our ability to be content or at peace?

[**Matthew**]: The chances of material things robbing us of contentment far outweighs the chance that they will bring us contentment. There's the famous quote of unknown origin that states, "The richest man is not he who has the most, but he who needs the least."

I remember the first time I walked the Camino in Spain. I started with a backpack weighing 20 pounds. As I was packing the backpack, I thought there's no way I can survive for a month or so with a backpack of merely 20 pounds. At the end of the first day, I ended up throwing stuff away or leaving stuff for other pilgrims. When I finally got to Santiago, the backpack might have been 10 pounds. And that included a handful of paperback books I had bought along the way. One of the greatest lessons of that experience was how profoundly liberating it was to walk into my home when I returned absolutely convinced that of all the things I possess in this world, I need very, very few.

It's a beautiful thing to be reminded how little we actually need. You commented about my paintings, and I do love art. You mentioned my books, and I would hate to live without books. That would be a real punishment. But for all the things I have been blessed to own and enjoy in this world, I'll never be confused again about what I need and what I don't need.

"All of us experience the sad effects of blind submission to consumerism. In the first place it represents crass materialism. At the same time, it represents a radical dissatisfaction because one quickly learns that the more one possesses, the more one wants, while deeper aspirations remain unsatisfied and perhaps even stifled."

- Pope John Paul II

[**Jack**]: Let's turn now to relationships.

What role do relationships, attachments to other people, have on our ability to be content or at peace?

[**Matthew**]: When relationships disquiet our contentment, we should go into that—there's a lot for us to learn. I think there's a holy discontentment and that's where people struggle. Most don't realize that discontentment and dissatisfaction can be a very holy thing.

I really believe that dissatisfaction gave us Francis of Assisi. It was his dissatisfaction that drove him to question his life, and the very meaning of life. He expressed many of the things people are expressing today: there must be more, I can give more, I can do more, I can be more. Many people are driven by ambition, but Francis was uniquely driven by dissatisfaction, and we know the result.

He is one of the most beloved people in history. And his admirers are not limited to Catholics, or even believers. Francis is loved and admired by all men and women of goodwill.

So, I guess, what I am trying to say is that there is a holy dissatisfaction. In fact, most spiritual conversions, using the word loosely because we're called to ongoing conversion, comes as we are grow increasingly dissatisfied with the current reality of our lives in particular and the world as a whole. It's that dissatisfaction that leads us deeper into the heart of God and the life of God.

"There's a difference between knowing God and knowing about God. When you truly know God, you have energy to serve Him, boldness to share Him, and contentment in Him."

- J. I. Packer

[Jack]: *Does the type of relationship have an influence on our ability to be content or at peace?*

[Matthew]: Interestingly enough, the more important a relationship is to us, the higher the chances of that relationship making us miserable and robbing us of our contentment. And we don't talk about that.

If there's someone I just sort of loosely know, it's easier for me to love that person than it is for me to love those closest to me. I am speaking of love as love in the purest sense of the word, the most universal sense. Love as willing the good of the other.

It is easy to love strangers in this way. I can desire every good thing for another person I don't know very well in a very detached way, because it doesn't really affect me. But then, in closer relationships, with the people I love the most, I want these people to grow, but at the same time there are things I may not want to change. And very often, when the people we love grow, that growth can be at odds with the ways we have become comfortable in that relationship. And so, in a selfish way, it can seem that their growth is at odds with what we desire for them, or for ourselves, or both. It's true in many intimate relationships, and I think it's true in relationships between parents and children.

Can we be content allowing our spouse, children, closest friends to grow, knowing that it will change our relationship with that person in unknown ways? It may be the best thing for the other person, it may be the best thing for your relationship with that person, but it may lead to an assault upon your personal preferences. And again, we are reminded that we don't always desire what is best for us or best for the people we love. It is easy to be selfish in any relationship.

[**Jack**]: There's no doubt about that.

Let's go in a slightly different direction. What's the relationship that dissatisfaction and contentment have with silence?

[**Matthew**]: I don't think you can get adequately in touch with either without silence. And I would add solitude. Like it or not, you sit in silence and solitude for long enough, and you're going to get in touch with your dissatisfaction or contentment, or both. I think it's impossible not to. If you sit long enough alone in quiet, you're going to get in touch with both. This is one of the reasons we are addicted to noise and distraction. We fear the truth and wisdom that silence inevitably and unavoidably reveals about who we are and how we are living our short lives on this earth.

> *"When we experience conflict or dissatisfaction, we are being called on to develop something in ourselves that is weak, hidden, or unknown."*
>
> *- Jett Psaris*

[Jack]: *If contentment and dissatisfaction were on the FBI's most wanted list, what would be public enemy number one?*

[**Matthew**]: Materialism. I think materialism would be public enemy number one for contentment. But not purely in a sort of "money and things" sense but more in the holistic sense that materialism is ultimately the rejection of spiritual realities. There's nothing in this world that can give you lasting contentment, nothing material. As I said earlier, contentment is not an outside reality, it's an inside reality. Materialism leads us deep into the mega-trend of soul denial that is consuming one generation after another at present. Once we deny the soul, we are inviting despair to sit at the head of the table of our lives, surrounded by disorientation, meaninglessness, and confusion.

Public enemy number one for dissatisfaction would likely be lack of self-awareness. When we don't know ourselves, and are not striving to know ourselves more with each passing year, we limit our ability to see the signs of life and to hear the gentle voice within us. What's behind that? Why are we so afraid to know ourselves? Why do we avoid ourselves? It would seem to me that anything we avoid we fear. But usually, our fears are non-specific, which makes them very hard to address or work with. This is often what we mean when we refer to fear of the unknown.

What do you think?

[**Jack**]: I would have said attachment to things for dissatisfaction. I wouldn't have said materialism for contentment. I was going to say noise or busyness for contentment. But that's, at best, a product of fear.

I think if you lead a life of regular solitude and silence, it's hard to go years and years without contending with dissatisfaction. It's really hard to do that. But it's a lot easier to avoid contending with your dissatisfaction when you're busy. You can basically numb yourself to what's happening inside of you. You don't have to pay attention to your dissatisfaction. I think that's why some people wake up in the midst of a mid-life crisis.

[**Matthew**]: Good insights. Distraction. Avoidance. It's more complex than that, but those are definitely ways a lot of people deal with dissatisfaction.

[**Jack**]: Exactly. In fact, for all of the topics, it's interesting to think about what's the greatest enemy of these things.

[**Matthew**]: I agree. It provides another way to look at things, a different perspective, which is very helpful, especially for those things that we need to examine regularly throughout our lives.

"True contentment is not having everything, but in being satisfied with everything you have."
- Oscar Wilde

[Five Ways to Foster Contentment]

Who is the richest person on earth today? Our minds tend to immediately go to those who have the most money when we hear that question. But is money the best gauge for the richness of a life? If you had to choose between having more money than you could ever need or the satisfaction that comes a well-lived life, which would you choose? Does the way you spend your time reflect this choice? Here are five simple ways to get started on the road to self-contentment.

1. **Stop comparing.**

   There are a lot of reasons why we should all stop comparing ourselves to other people. It is a thief of every form of happiness. The journey to contentment begins with the effort to become a-better-version-of-yourself moment by moment, each and every day. Contentment will never be found in trying to be any version of some other person or the version of yourself that you think other people want you to be.

2. **Count your blessings.**

   If you find it hard to eliminate comparisons, you're not alone. Sometimes, in order to stop doing something destructive, we have to replace it with something positive. A simple gratitude list can be that thing. Next time you sense yourself getting into comparison mode, stop and make a short list of five things you are grateful for. It can turn a whole day around. It is impossible to be content if you are not grateful.

3. **Spend time in silence and solitude.**

If you're serious about finding a sense of contentment in your life, spend time in silence and solitude. It is a non-negotiable. There you may find a sense of dissatisfaction or that something is missing in your life. This is a good thing. It's that sense of dissatisfaction that will guide you to discovering the very things standing between you and the contentment you seek.

4. **Look within.**

Contentment will never come from material things. It comes from within. Who you become is infinitely more important than what you do or what you have. Focus on becoming with a singleness of purpose, and peace and contentment will begin to flow in your life.

5. **Do good.**

For millennia, people have sought the secret to "the good life." They've wanted to know what type of life would lead to an ultimate sense of contentment and satisfaction. The answer has always been right in front of us: goodness itself. Fill your life with goodness—with love, kindness, gratitude, compassion, generosity—and you will fill it with contentment too.

Any contentment we experience in this life is just a taste, a foreshadowing, of the eternity God has prepared for us and yearns to share with you. Invite an eternal perspective into your daily decision making and you will taste the fruit of contentment more and more in this life.

The life that wants to live in you is different than the life you are living.

[guarding your heart]

being vigilant and discerning about who and what
you allow to dwell in your heart

[a bit of inspiration]

*For thousands of years, men and women of all faiths
have been making pilgrimages. These sacred journeys
are powerful experiences that people make in search
of God, His will, and His favor. Most of all, these sacred journeys remind us that life itself is a pilgrimage,
and that we are just passing through this place we call
earth. Many of these pilgrimages involve hundreds and
even thousands of miles of travel, and before modern
transportation they were grueling undertakings. But
contrary to popular belief, the longest and most difficult*

pilgrimage in the world has never been to Jerusalem or Santiago or Fatima.

The Sioux believed that the longest journey we can make in this life is from the head to the heart. This is also the longest spiritual journey we can make; it is the pilgrimage of prayer. We think of the heart as emotional, and it is, but it is also deeply spiritual. Are you living your life from the mind? Are you living your life from the heart? Or have you found the delicate balance between the heart and the mind that allows you to live in growing wisdom? Prayer helps us make the journey from the head to the heart, and it is prayer that allows us to balance the heart and mind so that we can live in wisdom.

Every journey has a series of ordinary moments, but there are other moments that stand out as significant. The significant moments on the pilgrimage of our lives usually present us with a choice that needs to be made. There is a great spiritual decision before you right now: To make prayer a daily habit in your life or not? This is a choice that will affect you every day for the rest of your life.

[Q & A with Matthew]

[**Jack**]: *To begin with, what do you mean by guarding your heart?*

[**Matthew**]: Guarding your heart is not about protecting yourself from never getting hurt. Guarding your heart is about guarding the life of God and the goodness within you, and about being vigilant and discerning about who and what you allow to dwell in your heart.

You are going to get hurt. Period. It is going to happen, it's unavoidable. As I said in *Life Is Messy*, Not only is it going to happen, but everyone who plays any significant role in your life is going to hurt you.

I know sitting here right now today, that I have been hurt by many people who are close to me, and I have also hurt them too.

We are human beings, we hurt each other. We do it mostly unconsciously, but it happens. Your heart is going to get hurt. We are not guarding our heart against getting hurt, otherwise you would never go anywhere, you would never talk to anyone, you would never do anything.

You are going to make yourself vulnerable, and the people you make yourself vulnerable to are going to hurt you. Hopefully they will love you in unimaginable ways also.

The goal of guarding our hearts is not to avoid being hurt. But it does mean we shouldn't be careless with our hearts or other people's.

The goal of guarding our hearts is to be vigilant about who and what we allow to come and dwell in our hearts. If you are going to admit someone into your heart, I think it helps to ask: Would you invite that person if God was coming to dinner at your place tonight? Because when you allow someone to enter your heart, you invite them to dwell with God in you.

So, the second piece of guarding our hearts is to guard the goodness that God has placed within you by keeping plenty of room available for God in your heart. If we allow the wrong people, things, and causes to occupy our hearts they will force God out.

"To love at all is to be vulnerable. Love anything, and your heart will certainly be wrung and possibly be broken. If you want to make sure of keeping it intact, you must give your heart to no one, not even to an animal. Wrap it carefully round with hobbies and little luxuries; avoid all entanglements; lock it up safe in the casket or coffin of your selfishness. But in that casket—safe, dark, motionless, airless—it will change. It will not be broken; it will become unbreakable, impenetrable, irredeemable."

- C.S. Lewis

[**Jack**]: *There's probably a fine line between vulnerability / loving generously and guarding your heart. Can you give me a sense of where that line is?*

[**Matthew**]: When guarding our heart against different things, we don't want our hearts to get hardened. There is a certain amount of pain, suffering, and maliciousness that would lead you to harden your heart, which is a protection mechanism.

Hardening your heart is a way of guarding your heart, but it's just the wrong way.

In being vulnerable, you have to analyze the risks to benefit ratio of that. For example, when I make myself vulnerable to my wife, the risk to benefit ration is off the charts to the upside. But if I make myself vulnerable to a stranger who's in a really difficult situation, that person may trample on my vulnerability. Or worse, for me, as a person in public life, they could take what is shared with them in a very sincere way, take it out of context, and use it to hurt me.

That doesn't mean we should be calculating every decision because we do need to listen to our hearts, but we should be using our hearts and minds when making decisions.

[**Jack**]: *Proverbs 4:23 says "Above all else, guard your heart for it determines the course of your life." That's a big statement, what do you think about that?*

[**Matthew**]: Well, I think it's true. I think we do it well at times and do it poorly at times. At times our hearts are filled with all things good, but at times we allow poisonous toxins into our hearts. That's what we struggle with: when you're there, how do you reverse that? You need a cleanse, or a spiritual cleanse.

The problem isn't that we let inner poisons or

toxins into our heart. We are all broken and that is okay. In *Life is Messy*, I wrote "But let me share with you the real problem with our brokenness. In our wasteful, consumption-addicted society, we throw broken things away. So we don't know what to do with our broken selves." I ultimately pose the question, "Can something that has been broken be put back together in a way that makes it more beautiful than ever before?"

There is a lot of guilt, shame, and self-loathing, especially around the idea that something can't be put back together. There is the false belief that if we allow our hearts to be filled with inner poisons and toxins, they cannot be cleansed. I don't believe that to be true. God wants to cleanse and soften our hearts so we can love deeply, and give us the wisdom to guard them against those poisons and toxins in the future.

> *"Above all else, guard your heart for it determines the course of your life."*
>
> - Proverbs 4:23

[Jack]: *What are some of the poisons and toxins that can fill your heart?*

[Matthew]: Any of the seven deadly sins, for a start: pride, greed, lust, envy, gluttony, anger, and sloth.

Unforgiveness of self and others figures high on the list. Judgment. Cynicism, too. It's okay to be skeptical, and in many ways it's healthy intellectually. I think our culture very often sees the virtues of being skeptical in cynicism, but that's misplacing them. Cynicism is particularly dangerous to the human heart.

The evidence is fairly clear if we return to an

early topic and look at cynicism and enthusiasm side-by-side. Cynical people tend to lack enthusiasm. You can be skeptical, intellectually skeptical, and still maintain great enthusiasm.

So, they are some of the things that poisons our hearts: Unforgiveness, judgement, cynicism, pride, greed lust, envy, gluttony, anger, sloth.

[Jack]: *When you're healthy and you're guarding your heart, what are you guarding?*

[**Matthew**]: When I was a kid, I saw this foreign movie with subtitles. I remember the family that were the main characters went to a Greek Orthodox Church and at Easter, each family took a candle home that was lit from the Paschal candle and then they lit a candle in their home which they kept constantly burning throughout the year.

In the movie, the little boy is sent to church by his dad because his mom is very sick. The boy was sent to church to bring the candle home, but he's a little kid and it was a stormy night, and when he came home, the candle had been blown out.

If you think about guarding an open flame, it requires astounding intentionality, constant vigilance, and peace of mind. And you can't be in a rush.

Anytime I need to slow down in life, this is an image that comes to me. I think to myself, okay slow down, you're in a crisis, but guard the flame. You have to move slowly; you have to move intentionally if you're going to guard that flame. You just can't rush around carelessly. So that's probably how I look at it.

The problem is, we do rush around carelessly. Some people's whole lives could be described that way. Tell me about his life: He spent his whole life rushing around carelessly. It's tragic when you put it in such start terms. It's arresting. But it happens at all the time. We need to decide with all the resolve we can muster not to live our lives that way.

[Jack]: *What is the equivalent to the flame within a person?*

[**Matthew**]: The presence of God. It's what I shared at the beginning and keep returning to: The life that wants to live in you is different than the life you are living. It's the divine life within us.

> *"To live is the rarest thing in the world. Most people exist, that is all."*
> - Oscar Wilde

[Jack]: *Jesus talks a lot about hardness of heart, especially when addressing the Pharisees, the religious elite of the time. What are your thoughts on that?*

[**Matthew**]: The Pharisees guarded their hearts in the wrong way by hardening their hearts, which prevented them from seeing God, especially how God was present in those in need. They paid the ultimate price that hardness of heart exacts, which is missing out on God moving in their life.

We can make the same mistake of guarding our hearts by hardening our hearts, which makes us miss out on seeing how God is moving in our lives.

Attachment is very important here. Going back to Proverbs 4:23: "Guard your heart, above all else, for it determines the course of your life." We can very easily translate that and bring more clarity to it by saying, whatever you attach your heart to will determine the course of your life.

We each need to ask ourselves regularly, what is your heart attached to?

Attachments and detachment each play a significant role in guarding your heart.

Empathy is huge, as is emotional intelligence.

The Pharisees lacked empathy. They were unwilling or unable to put themselves in other people's situation and feel their anxiety, stress, worry, or pain. This lack of empathy is unfortunately very common today.

[**Jack**]: As we talk about guarding your heart, it seems to me that we're talking about one of the hardest lessons of life to learn. Going back to what you said at the beginning, it's not about never getting hurt. You can't avoid that. The question is whether or not you can protect the life and love you were made for. And that's so hard.

If you could tell people just one or two practical exercises to help them guard their hearts, what would it be?

[**Matthew**]: The first is very simple: Slow down. Rushing through life we get distracting from what is happening within us in every sense. The second would be: Take time to meditate on the contents of your heart. What is currently occupying your heart, and what is your heart preoccupied with at present? We usually get preoccupied with someone or something before we allow it to come into our hearts. Look at the contents of your heart and do some spring cleaning.

[Five Ways to Guard Your Precious Heart]

Your heart is precious. It is precious to you and precious to God. It's important to be careful with it. Too often in our world we are encouraged to be thoughtless, careless, and even reckless with our own hearts and the hearts of other people. We see it in reality movies and television shows, social media gossip, and marriages steeped in disrespect. Careless hearts are a recipe for disaster in our relationships, but it also hinders our ability to become the-best-version-of-ourselves. It's time to change that. Here are five ways for you to reestablish vigilance and care of your heart.

1. **Pay attention to your thoughts.**

   The modern world is intent on separating the head from the heart. We want a neat box to put logic in and a separate one to put emotions in. But that's not how human beings work. Your head and your heart are intimately connected. What you allow into your mind, the content you consume, the gossip you listen to, the negative thoughts you harbor about another person... these spread like venom to your heart and determine the course of your life. Whatever you set your mind on will increase in your life. Set your mind on the higher things.

2. **Cultivate a strong voice within.**

An unguarded heart leads to one unavoidable outcome: regret. "If only I had made that choice," or "I wish I had taken action then," become too-constant refrains within an unguarded heart. But there is one proven way to live a life free of regret: develop and listen to your conscience. God has placed the voice of conscience within you because He wants you to have a guide to properly guarding your heart. Listen to it and you will live without regret.

3. **Reject the poisons of the heart.**

Holding onto emotions like anger, resentment, and unforgiveness is like drinking poison and expecting the other person to die. Have you been letting these poisons slowly constrict your capacity for life and goodness? When these emotions visit you, don't detain them any longer than necessary. Acknowledge them, learn the lesson they visited you to teach you, and then release them. Practice using the antidotes of forgiveness, kindness and gratitude. It's difficult, but it will fill you with life and hope.

4. **Trust actions more than words.**

There's an old writing adage, "Show, don't tell." Use this as a guide when deciding how much or how little to trust someone. Have they shown you they are trustworthy, or have they just told you they are? If you sense that someone is not worthy of your trust, or if someone has betrayed your trust in the past, you should guard your heart with extra vigilance from potential damage or manipulation.

5. **Have a strong support system.**

Guarding your heart can sound like a self-centered enterprise. It isn't. In fact, it is something you can't do alone. Rely on the people that have earned your trust. There will still be times when you get hurt or someone wounds your heart. Having people to turn to is key to healing and reviving your hope. A strong and healthy support system can ease the burden of guarding your heart by helping you evaluate and avoid dangerous situations and people.

God wants to help you have a strong and healthy heart. It's easy to forget that when we are experiencing emotional pain, when we've been betrayed, or when we've lost the ability to trust. But it's when we let go of our fear and anger that we can turn our attention to the good people God has placed in our lives, hear the inner voice He has placed inside us, and walk one step closer to the person He dreams we will become.

The life that wants to live in you is different than the life you are living.

[emotional boundaries]

rules of engagement for relationships; separating your feelings from the feelings of others; knowing what you are and are not responsible for

---

[a bit of inspiration]

Once, a psychology professor walked around his classroom full of students holding a glass of water with his arm straightened out to the side. He asked his students, "How heavy is this glass of water?"

The students started to shout out guesses–ranging anywhere from 4 ounces to one pound.

The professor replied, "The absolute weight of this glass isn't what matters while I'm holding it. Rather, it's the amount of time that I hold onto it that makes an impact.

"If I hold it for, say, two minutes, it doesn't feel like much of a burden. If I hold it for an hour, its weight may become more apparent as my muscles begin to tire. If I hold it for an entire day–or week–my muscles will cramp and I'll likely feel numb or paralyzed with pain, making me feel miserable and unable to think about anything aside from the pain that I'm in.

In all of these cases, the actual weight of the glass will remain the same, but the longer I clench onto it, the heavier it feels to me and the more burdensome it is to hold."

The class understood and shook their heads in agreement.

The professor continued to say, "This glass of water can represent a lot of things. It can represent the worries and stresses that you carry around with you every day. It can represent regret that you feel over things that you wish you did or didn't do. And it can be the burden you carry of boundaries violated again and again and again. If you think about them for a few minutes and then put them aside, it's not a heavy burden to bear. If you think about them a little longer, you *will start to feel the impacts of the stress. If you carry you these things with you all day, you will become incapacitated, prohibiting you from doing anything else until you let them go."*

It's time to return to a right relationship with your worries, your stresses, your past, the people in your life. Don't give them your entire attention while your life is passing you by.

[Q & A with Matthew]

[**Jack**]: *What is so important about emotional boundaries that you would make it one of the topics?*

[**Matthew**]: This is one of the areas where nobody I know is exempt from need of reclaiming. Most of us have had our emotional boundaries violated, and most of us have violated our own emotional boundaries.

One aspect that is important to note about emotional boundaries is that they are massively violated at this time in history. Most people don't have a good sense of what they are. Most people don't have healthy emotional boundaries. Most people have had emotional boundaries violated significantly and are either unaware that it actually happened or have no idea what to do about it. You could argue it is a form of guarding your heart, but it is both distinct and important enough to be dealt with separately. I think there is a strong connection between the two, but they are not identical. Especially when you consider the way boundaries should guide the way we engage with others in all manner of relationships.

There are three aspects to emotional boundaries that I am considering in this conversation. The first surrounds the rules of engagement for relationships. The second involves separating your feelings from the feelings of other people. And the third is know what you are and are not responsible for.

The simplest example of the rules of engagement aspect is a neighbor who is constantly showing up at your home unannounced and uninvited. This person is violating not only common courtesy and etiquette, but also your emotional boundaries.

Sometimes in order to separate your feelings from the feelings of other people, you need space to explore how you are really feeling. When something happens our hearts and minds get flooded with thoughts and ideas, ours, and others. We immediately have a sense of how other people will feel about what just happened. This is the emotional intelligence we call empathy. It is a beautiful thing, but not if we skip over our own thoughts and feelings and go straight to other people's. If you are having trouble separating your feelings from how other people feel about a situation, you may need space to process. If you ask someone to give you space and they don't, they are infringing on your emotional boundaries.

When we are unable to separate our feelings

from other people's feelings, we lose sight of what we need and want.

The third aspect is knowing what you are and are not responsible for. An example we are all familiar with here is when someone apologizes for something they had nothing to do with. Apologizing is an important part of any relationship because it communicates that we care and that we take responsibility for our words and actions. When we apologize for things other people should be apologizing for, or for things that are not anyone's fault, the lines get blurry.

Many people apologize incessantly for things they had nothing to do. It is a nervous or anxious response for many people. It's okay to be sorry that something happened, or that someone had to go through something, but it's important that we are clear in our minds and words that we are not responsible for these situations.

The reason setting emotional boundaries is so important is because without them we can easily

lose our sense of self and then we become suscep-
tible to being used and manipulated by others for
their own selfish purposes.

[Jack]: *How do we learn about emotional boundaries?*

[**Matthew**]: I think it's important to understand
that many people live their whole lives without
hearing the term. But we are trained as children
about emotional boundaries, and boundaries in
general. This training is informal and organic, but
every day and powerful.

The problem is that our training is always
flawed. Even the best parents are not perfect. The
idea that we're not going to have some negative
impact on our children is the foolish. It is usually
unconscious, but it occurs nonetheless. Our own
woundedness impacts the way we parent our children, and that is more manifest in the emotional
realm than any other.

It is probably easiest to understand this topic by looking at how emotional boundaries have been violated. There are some stereotypical examples, such as parents who just show up at their adult children's home and take over. They treat their son or daughter like a little child, even though they are now grown adults with their own family.

[**Jack**]: *Is there another way to explore this topic and gain insight to how it might be impacting our relationships today?*

[**Matthew**]: Yes. Absolutely. If you really want to delve into it, I would encourage you to explore the first contract of your life. This contract is usually between parents and their children, though it could be between you and whoever raised you. This question is the essence of the first contract: What did you have to do as a child to receive love?

If love was given or withheld from you as a child based on whether or not you did as you were told, you are probably still operating out of that paradigm at some level. Or you may be operating out of the extreme opposite paradigm. You may refuse to do what the other person wants in every instance, testing the other person, telling yourself, "If he really loves me, he will let me do whatever I want." Extremes tend to be unhealthy in relationships, especially when they involve games and tests, we have set up in our minds and not told the other person about.

If as a child you had to get great grades or make the team or be the best, in order to receive love, you are probably still living out of that paradigm at some level. It may in your deep subconscious, but somewhere deep inside you probably think that accomplishing things makes you lovable.

The most important thing to remember if we want to overcome the imbalance of these early emotional contracts is that the person you are with today is not your mother, father, or whoever your primary guardian was as a child.

> *"Walls keep everybody out. Boundaries teach them where the door is."*
>
> - Mark Groves

[**Jack**]: *Could you elaborate further on what you mean by what you had to do to get love as a child?*

[**Matthew**]: We can ask ourselves and reflect on what we needed to do to get love when we were growing up. It may be challenging or uncomfortable, but the truth is that it forms very ingrained circuitry in our brains and in our hearts. We learn, "If I do X, I will receive love, and if I don't love may be withheld." And our need for love is primary and indispensable, so these early lessons ingrain themselves powerful in our psyche.

Some parents teach their children that they will receive love, if they do what they are told to do. The number of emotional boundaries that have been violated in that contract between a parent and a child very early is astounding. That person has little chance of establishing healthy emotional boundaries as an adult unless he or she really explores the impact these rules had on them and continue to have.

Many parents, consciously or subconsciously, give love based on accomplishment. If you observed this and pointed it out, they might say that is ridiculous. But as I say, many are oblivious to. What they are doing and how they are doing it. It could be as simple as what we affirm and encourage, or what we praise. Affirmation, encouragement, and praise are powerful in the life of a child. So powerful that what we choose as parents to praise and affirm can determine the direction of their lives. Millions of people choose careers based on the fact that when they took an interest in that area as a child they received more praise, affirmation, and encouragement than any other time in their childhood.

As a parent, I know that it's so easy to fall into that trap.

One year my daughter really struggled in school. I was not concerned, and I encouraged her not to be concerned. "Keep working hard, we all learn at different speeds." One of the earliest examples of this is that babies learn to walk between 8 and 18 months. That's a huge variable, but when they show up at school, we expect them all to learn everything, in every subject, in lock step.

The following year when Isabel's report card came she was beaming. When I came home it was clear that she had received congratulations from a group of people who were at the house that evening.

When Isabel came down to my office for story time and to chat before she went to bed, she asked, "Daddy you didn't say anything about my grade?" I replied, "I was waiting for this time we have together to talk to you about your report card. There were lots of other people around and I wanted our conversation to be special."

"Are you proud of my grade?" she asked.

"No," I said, and I saw her face fall a little. "I'm proud of how hard you worked. We have talked before about grades. If you work hard and foster your love of learning, it really doesn't matter much to me if you are first or last in the class, because I know of you do your best, keep working hard, and decide to learn a little every day for the rest of your life you will live a rich and full life."

"Are you happy I got a good grade?" she pressed.

"I am, baby. I am so happy for you. I am happy that all your hard work and perseverance was rewarded. But what impresses me the most is how you invested in yourself and worked hard even though it was difficult."

I could see she was unsure. Even as young as she is, it seemed too good to be true, and that made me sad because it was proof that other value systems are already forming in her.

"Give me a hug," I said. She wrapped her long arms around my neck, and I whispered in her ear, "I love you so much, baby. I want you to know that you don't have to do anything to earn my love. It is already yours. When you work hard at school and do well, you give yourself that gift. When you get good grades, it's natural to feel warm and happy inside, but whether you get an 'A' or an 'F,' I love you the same. That doesn't change. There will be times when you disappoint me and disappoint yourself, times when I make you unhappy and times when you make me unhappy, but that doesn't mean I love you less. I love you always. There are many things you will be unsure about in your life, but my love for you shouldn't be one of them. I love you no matter what."

She was still hugging me, with her head nestled into me, and I felt her smile on my neck. It was one of the most delightful feelings I have ever experienced.

The thing is, I know that in little conversations like those, if I affirm the grade, the grade becomes the most important thing. And I don't want to set my children up to chase outcomes, however good. I want to help them develop the skills and character necessary to respond to the opportunities life sets on their doorstep.

It's in these little conversations that we knowingly or unknowingly tell our children what we really care about. In the process we're telling them and teaching them what they have to do to be loved—and they will carry this into every relationship for the rest of their lives. So, we need to avoid at all costs is saying something that sounds to them like, "I love you when you..." or "I love you if you..."

"You don't have to do anything to receive my love. It is already yours." What does this do? It helps them develop a sense of self knowing they are valued, not for what they have or what they can do, but simply for who they are—sons and daughters of God.

That's how God loves. It is the model of love that he lays before us in the Gospels and the ultimate model of parental love.

We don't have to do anything to get God's love.

It is given freely and without limitation. As parents we should strive to model this love to our children.

There will be times when I disagree with what my children do, there will be times when I am disappointed with them. Just as there are plenty of times when God disagrees with what I have done and disappointed with my choices. But that doesn't mean He stops loving me. This sets our children up for a completely different emotional experience of life.

"When trying to teach someone a boundary, they learn less from the enforcement of the boundary and more from the way the boundary was established."

- *Bryant H. McGill*

[**Jack**]: That makes me think about my little boy. He loves playing basketball on the hoop in our house. He can reach the hoop and dunk, so that's what he does, he just jams it in there. And I noticed that when he misses, he just goes and picks up the ball, but when he actually dunks it, he turns to me and starts clapping. I realized that was a powerful reflection back to me. Like, I only clap when he is successful.

It made me think, what message is that sending him about my love for him? So, I just started clapping every time I knew he was intentionally trying to do it. But in some ways, it's already a script written somewhere in his mind. It takes an intentional effort on my part to shift that script.

I guess that leads me to another question.

When you have long established boundaries that exist, healthy or unhealthy, how do you establish new ones?

[**Matthew**]: I think it's very important to realize that this happens to everybody. For example, almost everybody has to renegotiate new boundaries with their parents at some point.

And it is a messy business. If you said to your parents, "I feel like you love me more when I do what you want me to do," most parents would be horrified at the idea. They would think this is outrageous and delusional, that they love you always, no matter what. But tell them you are not coming for Thanksgiving this year (as an example) and their reaction would tell a different story.

It is crucial to understand that you can't change other people. You can only change how you respond to them. Only you can establish new boundaries.

[**Jack**]: *What's the first step in establishing new boundaries?*

[**Matthew**]: Not sure there is one definitive step.

And if this is something someone is struggling with, they should read more or speak with a professional. But here are my off-the-cuff thoughts.

The first step to establishing new boundaries is to put yourself in right relationship with the other person or people. This needs to be reality bound. Many parents for example continue to see their children as children even long into their adult lives. It's important to remind yourself, "I am not a child anymore."

The next step is to tell the other person, or people. This can be hard, but it is much harder to establish new boundaries if the other person doesn't know. Not impossible, but much harder.

Once you establish new boundaries, point out as soon as they are crossed. Do it however you are comfortable with, but don't ignore the violation or avoid the confrontation. If you ignore or avoid it, you will be back where you were before, likely feeling even worse about yourself than you did before you realized you needed to make a change.

> *"Daring to set boundaries is about having the courage to love ourselves even when we risk disappointing others."*
>
> - *Brené Brown*

[**Jack**]: Some people may be unfamiliar with the idea of emotional boundaries. Others may be opposed, suggesting that setting boundaries is selfish.

Is setting boundaries selfish?

[**Matthew**]: Absolutely not. It reminds me actually of the common attack of the phrase "become the best-version-of-yourself." People sometimes say that's selfish.

But I think the argument can be made almost indisputably that the best thing I can do for my spouse, my children, my friends, my colleagues, my employees, and everyone else on the planet is to become a-better-version-of-myself. Every time I do, even in the smallest way, everyone benefits from that. So, no, it is not selfish. Quite the opposite in fact, it is a way of preparing to love people more and better.

That's like saying growing in holiness is selfish. I have always seen the two, becoming the best-version-of-yourself and growing in holiness, as synonymous and inseparable.

Setting boundaries is not selfish either. Establishing healthy emotional boundaries is a great gift to give ourselves, and it is a gift that allows us to help our friends and family develop healthy emotional boundaries also.

"Boundary setting helps you prioritize your needs over other people's wants."

- *Lauren Kenson*

[Five Ways to Establish Healthy Emotional Boundaries]

Do you ever wish that relationships came with a manual? It might solve a lot of problems. While our relationships may never come with an actual manual, we do have the ability to clearly define, adapt, and defend our emotional boundaries. When we don't, it often leads to frustration, resentment, pain and mistrust. But if we can muster the courage to establish healthy emotional boundaries, it will change the way we value ourselves, protect us from resentment, and allow us to build dynamic relationships of every type. If it's time to examine your emotional boundaries, here are five ways.

1. Find an objective voice.

You have a unique and central perspective on your relationships. But it's a perspective shaped by your emotions, your past, your hopes, and

your fears. That makes it hard to objective-
ly evaluate your relationships in general and
boundaries specifically. Find someone you trust
to be honest and objective and ask that person
to help you see your relationships more clearly. This will help you develop a healthy level
of self-awareness and avoid unnecessary guilt,
which are key to emotional boundary setting.

2. **Start small.**

Whether you are trying to re-establish boundaries or setting them for the first time, don't
bite off more than you can chew. This is not an
all-or-nothing enterprise. It's also not a once-
and-done situation. You establish boundaries over time. And over time you tweak them
as you become more aware of the dynamics
of a particular relationship. Start small. Simply learning to say 'no' in situations can have
a huge impact on re-establishing boundaries.
And don't forget, if you don't feel free to say
'no', you are not free to say 'yes.'

3. **Beware of social media.**

   Social media is a lawless land when it comes to emotional boundaries. It makes it easier than ever for people to violate one another's boundaries from a distance without facing immediate or lasting consequences. That's abundantly clear in the incredible amount of gossip that exists on social media. Gossip violates all kinds of emotional boundaries, dehumanizes people, destroys reputations, and ruins relationships. Know your own limits and the invisible nature of boundaries on social media.

4. **Be consistent.**

   It's hard to hit a moving target. If you allow your boundaries to shift unnecessarily, it will confuse others and potentially encourage unwanted behaviors. Give other people the best chance to respect your boundaries by keeping them clear and consistent.

5. **Respect other people's boundaries.**

   This is the golden rule of emotional boundaries: Treat other people's emotional boundaries the way you want your boundaries to be treated. If you don't, you may give others a sense that they can violate your boundaries too.

You can have healthy emotional boundaries. And you deserve to. When they have been violated or remain unclear, it's easy to believe we will never find a way to reestablish worthy emotional boundaries. Focusing on these five things will allow you to take the first steps back toward healthy emotional boundaries and give you the confidence you need to defend them. Relationships don't come with a manual, but setting healthy emotional boundaries can help you build relationships that flourish and last.

The life that wants to live in you is different than the life you are living.

[love of learning]

an ongoing desire for unique opportunities to learn

[a bit of inspiration]

When my eldest son, Walter, first went to school, his teacher asked me what my hopes were regarding his education. I told her: "I don't really care if he learns to read first in his class or last in his class; eventually he will learn to read. I want you to work with us to instill in him a love for learning."

If children develop a love for learning, their curiosity and creativity are fostered, and they will become lifelong learners—and continuous learners tend to be successful at everything they turn their attention to.

Wherever you find excellence, you find continuous learning. They go hand in hand. Wherever you find continuous learning missing, you usually find mediocrity.

I've been blessed to know some amazing people in this world. Some of the best in the world in their fields. When you get to know the best of the best at anything, you discover that they are insanely persistent at learning more about their craft. I have seen it in great actors and musicians, and I have seen it in great golfers and authors. I have seen it in artists, entrepreneurs, sailors, chefs, and tech geniuses.

Whatever your age, if you have not yet fallen in love with learning, begin that love affair today. Here are ten inspiring quotes to help you get started!

1. *"A love of learning has a lot to do with learning that we are loved." - Fred Rogers*
2. *"Anyone who stops learning is old, whether at twenty or eighty. Anyone who keeps learning stays young." - Henry Ford*
3. *"The beautiful thing about learning is nobody can take it from you." - B.B. King*
4. *"Love of learning is the most necessary passion... in*

it lies our happiness. It is a sure remedy for what ails us, an unending source of pleasure." - Emilie du Châtelet

5. *"Learning is a treasure that will follow its owner everywhere." - Chinese Proverb*

6. *"Love of learning will never let you down. You can have a quest for money, you can have a quest for power, you can have a quest for fame, and they are sometimes gratifying and sometimes self-destructive. The love of learning is always gratifying and never self-destructive." - David McCullough*

7. *"The love of money and the love of learning rarely meet." - English Proverb*

8. *"An investment in knowledge always pays the best interest." - Ben Franklin*

9. *"Education is the key to unlock the golden door of freedom." - George Washington Carver*

10. *"The capacity to learn is a gift; the ability to learn is a skill; the willingness to learn is a choice." - Brian Herbert*

[Q & A with Matthew]

[**Jack**]: Love of learning may not have made many people's list of aspects of their life that they need to reclaim.

Why did love of learning make your list?

[**Matthew**]: It made my list because most people are not continuous learners. And yet, it's a crucial aspect of human flourishing.

Love of learning fuels enthusiasm and shines light on areas of dissatisfaction. You're more likely to recognize problems with emotional boundaries, for example, if you're continuously learning. So, I think it's interconnected with the other areas of life we are talking about reclaiming. And in some ways, it holds everything together, or keeps everything alive.

More than that, we are increasingly becoming a culture of non-readers. As we do, I think the quality of life, quality of our relationships, quality and focus of our conversations, and the quality of our decisions are all diminishing.

Love of learning is essential to my life. I do it almost unconsciously in many ways, every day. Oftentimes when asked to do a task or solve a problem, people sit down and try to find the answer in their own minds. But continuous learners don't do that. They have learned that someone has done almost anything we set out to do, and they study the best practices that have been established. They get a book, search online, and survey the landscape. What they don't do is sit there starring at a blank sheet of paper.

> *"Live as if you were to die tomorrow. Learn as if you were to live forever."*
> – *Mahatma Gandhi*

[Jack]: *How do people lose a love of learning?*

[Matthew]: Very often it happens as a result of a negative experience at school. Unfortunately, it's quite common, especially with how our education system is focused on grades and achievement.

I'm familiar with the woeful loss of the love of learning because that happened to me. I could not spell when I was about seven, so I had to repeat the first grade. And a lot of bullying and teasing came with that. And then in second grade, I had a really nasty teacher and I just disengaged and lost my love of learning.

It didn't come back until I was about 15. I used to work in a pharmacy every day after school, where I would ride my bike around delivering packages, mostly to elderly or sick people. Those who couldn't get to the pharmacy to get the medication. The pharmacist I worked for there was a fabulous person. I would come after school on my bike, and I'd walk into the back of the pharmacy, and he'd send me to get two chocolate milkshakes at this place across the street. So I went to get the milkshakes and then we would stand around at the back of the pharmacy. He would just talk to me. He would ask me questions. He would challenge every assumption, even if he agreed with it, he'd ask why is that true? "Are you really sure that's true?" he'd say, "What about this?" "What about that?"

Through these conversations, he gave me a great gift. He gave me back my love of learning. It completely changed my school career from about the age of 15. I absolutely would not be sitting here, I would not have been able to do what God has allowed me to do in the last 30 years without the influence of many people, but in respect of the love of learning, he really sparked that again for me. It's an amazing gift to give somebody.

[**Jack**]: *Are some people born with it?*

[**Matthew**]: Maybe. I don't know. It is probably there in the curiosity of every child, but we tend to lose it. And once lost, I think you need to be taught it. Someone who doesn't have it probably has never been around someone who had it.

"Wisdom is not a product of schooling but of the lifelong attempt to acquire it."

- Albert Einstein

[**Jack**]: *How do you live out this love of learning in your own life?*

[**Matthew**]: I love books, but I especially love audiobooks. I listen to audiobooks every day. It's been a huge part of my life and has been since I first started traveling. I'm a very slow reader, so even when

I want to read a book and underline it, very often, I'll have the book and I'll listen to the audio at the same time. It helps to keep me focused and not spend too much time on a page. Sometimes I can get lost in a sentence, a single idea might swallow me, or I might just be fascinated with the structure of a sentence or word choice, and the next thing I know I have read the same sentence 20 times.

I'm always reading lots of books. I'll have a business book going, a novel going, a spiritual book or two going, and I am usually reading a biography. The variety feeds my creativity. What I find interesting is how it has evolved over time. For the first five or six years after my reversion I read spiritual books almost exclusively.

In my early 20s I started reading biographies and autobiographies and I became addicted to them. And what they taught me is that there is an arc of a person's life. There are ups and downs. You see these incredibly famous people who've done extraordinary things and you realize their life is messy too. They had critics and detractors. They had faults and failings, and flaws and defects, and they worked on them and or made peace with them, or whatever they could do to keep moving the ball forward in their life.

And so, by looking at a person's whole life, it gave me a maturity that I didn't have. I think it informed the way I wrote and spoke, and I think it informed the way I live my life. So that was one way learning has been life-changing.

Before I was in my 30s, I never read much fiction, but then I started reading fiction in my 30s and I think that shows in my writing. I think there was a shift around that time because I got much more in touch with humanity through fiction. My empathy developed, you know when I wrote *The Rhythm of Life* I was very idealistic, and so very young, and my attitude was essentially, if you have a problem, fix it. If you're failing at something, work through it. This was my paradigm because that's how I had lived my life.

But inevitably you come up against things in life that you cannot fix. Things you have to live with, and these things are messy. So, I think fiction made me a lot more empathetic and got me in touch with my humanity. It got me in touch with other people's humanity and it changed the nature of how I approach meeting people where they are and leading them to where God is calling them to be. Fiction helped me do that in a way that I think would surprise many people. I don't think many people would think fiction helped me work that out, but fiction shows you how messy life is.

"It's not that I don't like people. It's just that when I'm in the company of others—even my nearest and dearest—there always comes a moment when I'd rather be reading a book."
- Maureen Corrigan

[**Jack**]: *On the topic of books, you've said, "Tell me the books you're reading in the next 12 months, and I will tell you what your life will look like in a year." Can you be that bold?*

[**Matthew**]: I think you can. We definitely become the books that we read. It is not just entertainment. And I've expanded that concept since I wrote that line 25 years ago to say we become the content we consume, because we are consuming most of our content today in new forms through new platforms.

I also think the reverse is true. I think you could look at a person today and probably fairly accurately predict what content they've consumed in the last year, last 5 years, or 10 years of their lives.

> *"Anyone who stops learning is old, whether at twenty or eighty. Anyone who keeps learning stays young. The greatest thing in life is to keep your mind young."*
>
> *– Henry Ford*

[Jack]: *Where can someone start with reading who hasn't picked up a book in years or even decades?*

[Matthew]: Read five pages a day. Don't think about the lost time, just begin today. Five pages a day for ten years is almost 300 books. If you read 300 great books over the next ten years, your life is going to change radically and for the better. You will be amazed, no astounded, how this one habit reaches into every other aspect of your life. What we read today walks and talks with us tomorrow.

[Five Ways to Fall in Love with Learning]

The day you fall in love with learning is the day your life changes forever. Why? Because from that moment forward, you never stop growing. From then on, your life will be filled with the inspiration and wisdom you need to flourish. You will never find life boring. If you've never fallen in love with learning, then welcome to a whole new world. If you've lost your love of learning or had it stripped away over time, here are five ways you can fall in love all over again!

1. **Do something you loved to do as a child.**
    Most of us can remember a time when we were young and had an insatiable curiosity. What did you love to do or explore as a child? Was there something you wanted to do with your life but were discouraged from doing it? Read on that topic. Get back in touch with that passion in some small way. Doing that activity or explor-

ing that aspect of the world again will trigger the curiosity you felt as a child, and you will carry that spark into other aspects of your life!

2. **Make a list of things you would love to learn to do.**

   You've got your to-do list. We keep track of the tasks, chores, and responsibilities we need to complete. It's just as important to be intentional about our dreams and passions. Generate a list tonight of things you would truly love to learn. Make sure your list has something you can get started on tomorrow with little to no cost. But put a couple of things on the list that seem impossible too. Let life surprise you.

3. **Ask great questions.**

   Our lives are a response to the questions we ponder. Great questions snap our attention into focus, bring great clarity, and allow us to see things in a way we have never seen them before. Develop the habit of asking questions of yourself, of others, and of life. Everyone knows more about one topic than any other topic. Find out what that topic is and start asking them questions. You will learn an astounding amount about that person, that topic, the world, and yourself.

4. **Schedule time to read.**

Schedule the most important things, not just the urgent things. Because the more important things are hardly ever urgent. You are never going to wake up and say to yourself, "I urgently need to read today." Books change our lives. Don't make it one of those things you hope to get around to. Put it on your schedule. Make it a habit. Try to do it at the same time every day. If you don't schedule time, it probably won't happen!

5. **Stay curious.**

Curiosity expands our world. A question as simple as, "Are you reading any good books at the moment?" can expand your world every day. It's fascinating to hear about what people are reading, and often they can summarize the main points in two or three sentences or ideas. This is great, because let's face it, we don't have time to read all the books we would like to.

It's a tragedy when a person never develops a love of learning in life. And it's concerning how quickly and completely our love of learning can be stripped away as we grow older. Each of these five suggestions has the potential to inject your life with a new level of passion and energy. Hopefully they are just the beginning of a much longer and more exciting journey propelled by a true love of learning!

The life that wants to live in you is different than the life you are living.

[reclaiming our souls in a secular world]

where our spiritual self resides and where our spiritual self encounters God

---

[a bit of inspiration]

Once upon a time on a glorious summer's evening, in an ancient English castle in the hills on the outskirts of London, there was a banquet.

More than six hundred guests had traveled from all over the world to attend this lavish affair. There were movie stars and musicians, artists and politicians, princes and princesses, fashion designers and beautiful models, men and women who owned businesses large enough to be small countries, and a handful of others, of no particular note, who had endeared themselves to the host over the years.

The evening was to be celebrated not with music, or speeches, or dancing, but with a presentation by a famous Shakespearean actor.

The castle was radiant, adorned with a springtime of flowers and perfectly lit with a myriad of candles. The people enjoyed a sumptuous meal and a wonderful selection of the finest wines the world had to offer.

When the guests had finished their dinner, but before dessert was served, the host stood up and welcomed them. He then explained, "This evening, instead of music, and speeches, and dancing, I have invited England's most celebrated Shakespearean actor to perform for us." The people graciously applauded, and the actor stood, moved toward the center of the banquet hall, and began to speak.

He spoke eloquently and powerfully. For thirty-five minutes he moved about the banquet hall, brilliantly reciting famous passages from the writings of William Shakespeare.

"Oh, I am but fortune's fool . . ."

"To be or not to be—that is the question:
Whether 'tis nobler in the mind to suffer
The slings and arrows of outrageous fortune
Or to take arms against a sea of troubles . . ."

"Shall I compare thee to a summer's day?
Thou art more beautiful and more temperate . . ."

"Neither a borrower nor a lender be,
for loan oft loses both itself and a friend.
And borrowing dulleth the edge of husbandry.
This above all, to thine own self be true,
And it must follow as night follows day
Thou canst not then be false to any man."

After each brief episode the audience erupted in ap-
plause, and their applause echoed up through the castle
and spilled out into the moonlit courtyards.

"'Tis but thy name that is my enemy: Thou art thyself . . . What's in a name? That which we call a rose by any other name would smell as sweet;

So Romeo would, were he not Romeo call'd, Retain thy dear perfection which he owes..."

"If we shadows have offended,
Think but this and all is mended,
That you have but slumbered here
While these visions did appear . . ."

With this, the closing passage from A Midsummer Night's Dream, the actor took a bow and announced that he was finished. The guests clapped and cheered and called for an encore. The actor rose to his feet once more to oblige his eager audience. "If anyone has a favorite Shakespearean passage, if I know it, I would be happy to recite it," he said.

Several people spontaneously raised their hands. One man asked for the soliloquy from Macbeth. Another asked for the balcony scene from Romeo and Juliet.

And then a young woman asked for Sonnet 14. One after the other, the actor brought these passages to life—boldly, brilliantly, tenderly, thoughtfully, each excerpt matched perfectly with its corresponding emotion.

Now an elderly gentleman toward the back of the banquet hall raised his hand and the actor called on him. As it turned out, the old man was a priest. "Sir," he said, standing in his place to be heard, "I realize it's not Shakespeare, but I was wondering if you would recite for us the twenty-third Psalm."

The actor paused and looked down as if he were remembering some event far in the past, perhaps a moment in his childhood. Then he smiled and spoke up. "Father, I would be happy to recite the Psalm on just one condition, and that is, when I am finished, you too will recite the Psalm for us here tonight."

The priest was taken aback. He hesitated. He was a little embarrassed now and, looking down, he fidgeted with the tablecloth. But he really wanted to hear the actor recite the Psalm. So finally, he smiled and agreed. "Very well."

The crowd hushed in anticipation and the actor began in his powerful and eloquent voice. "The Lord is my shepherd, there is nothing I shall want . . ."

When the actor finished reciting the Psalm the audience rose to their feet in ovation. They clapped and cheered as if they would never stop, and their adulation again echoed through the castle and out into the midsummer's evening.

After what seemed like several minutes, the guests finally settled and returned to their seats. Then the actor looked down the banquet hall to where the old priest was sitting and said, "Father, it's your turn now."

As the priest stood up at his table a whirl of whispers raced around the room. Shifting in his place, the old priest looked down, placed one hand on the table to steady himself, and took a deep breath.

A look of vivid recollection came across his face. He seemed to slip away to some other place. Then in a voice that was gentle and deeply reflective, he began.

"The Lord is my shepherd,

there is nothing I shall want.

He lets me lie down in green pastures.

He leads me beside peaceful waters.

He restores my soul.

He guides me along the way of righteousness as be-fits his name.

Even though I walk through the valley of the shad-ow of death,

I will not be afraid. For the Lord is at my side. His rod and his staff comfort and protect me.

He prepares a table for me in the presence of my enemies.

He anoints my head with oil.

My cup overflows.

Surely goodness and mercy will follow me all the days of my life. And I will live in the house of the Lord, forever."

When the priest was finished not a sound could be heard in the banquet hall. Nobody clapped, nobody moved, and nobody spoke. A profound silence had descended upon the castle. Women wiped tears from their eyes. Men sat staring openmouthed. A tear slipped from the eye of the host. And as the humble old priest gently sat down, every set of eyes in the banquet hall was fixed upon him.

The faces of the guests radiated awestruck amazement. The actor was perplexed. He wondered why the priest's gentle words had touched the people so deeply. Then like a shaft of light passing across his face, it dawned on him.

Seizing the moment, the actor stood up and said, "My friends, do you realize what you have witnessed here tonight?" They gazed back at him with a communal stare of wonderment. They knew they had witnessed something profound, but were uncertain of its meaning. The actor continued, "Why was the old priest's recital of the Psalm so much more powerful than my own? As I see it, the difference is this: I know the Psalm, but Father, he knows the Shepherd."

Get to know the Shepherd. Stop trying to put together a master plan for your life and for your happiness.

Instead, seek out the Master's plan for your life and for your happiness. Allow him to lead you, to guide you, to be your companion, your friend, your coach, and your mentor. He will lead you to green pastures. He will restore your soul. And your cup will overflow.

[Q & A with Matthew]

[**Jack**]: We'll start with an easy one (laughs)... *define the soul.*

[**Matthew**]: (Laughs) Great philosophers like Aristotle and Socrates all struggled to define the soul, so I won't get too deep into what it is or what it isn't, but it is where our spiritual self resides. It is where our spiritual self communes with God; where God chooses to reside in us. It is where the best of who you are and the best of what you do emanates from.

The idea that God dwells within us is a firm tenant of Christianity, though is an often ignored or purposely avoided element of Christianity. But it is essential to right relationship with God.

> *"The Lord can leave us wanting relative to certain things (sometimes judged indispensable in the eyes of the world), but He never leaves us deprived of what is essential: His presence, His peace and all that is necessary for the complete fulfillment of our lives, according to His plans for us."*
> - Jacques Philippe

[**Jack**]: There's one line that's relevant here that I don't think I've ever heard a homily preached on, but it's one of Jesus' more striking sayings. Jesus says, "And do not fear those who kill the body but cannot kill the soul. But rather fear Him who is able to destroy both soul and body in hell." In your last statement you said the soul is synonymous with the best in you.

Destroying the soul is destroying the best in you, so what destroys the soul?

[**Matthew**]: Alienation from God, which I talked about in *I Heard God Laugh*, is alienation from self. And that is what the current age has not worked out.

This is where the chaos and confusion is coming from. We have actually alienated ourselves from all the best aspects of ourselves. The moral, emotional, psychological, spiritual implications of this alienation from God and self are massive. The repercussions are literally unending.

Rejection of God destroys the soul. Unforgiveness is a close second. I think the runaway trains of any of the seven deadly sins we talked about earlier destroy the soul.

Addiction is before us more and more it seems, and a form of soul destruction. It is like a form of modern demonic possession. In Jesus's time, the erratic and destructive behavior of an addict would have been considered caused by demonic possession.

And then there are things we do to ourselves, like shame, avoidance, unresolved guilt, or unacknowledged guilt.

Destroy is a pretty strong word. In most of our spiritual problems, they're not so complete or incomplete. They are more gradual, more incremental. Ignoring the voice of conscience will ultimately destroy the soul, but it tends to happen very gradually.

And you don't wake up one day and say, oh my soul is destroyed. I think we recognize at times, I am less soulful. And I think that's important to monitor. There are times when I am more soulful in my work, other times when I am less soulful in my work. And it's important to recognize that more times when I'm more soulful as a parent, as a husband, as a friend.

> *"We are not human beings having a spiritual experience. We are spiritual beings having a human experience."*
> – Pierre Teilhard de Chardin

[**Jack**]: You've discussed the idea of a content diet before. It's a term some people may be unfamiliar with.

What do you mean by a content diet?

[**Matthew**]: Well, when I'm trying to really understand something, I often employ a tactic called the wisdom of the opposite. And I think that's really powerful here.

A question I've been thinking about lately is: If you wanted to destroy a person, and you could only do one thing, but you couldn't touch them or harm them physically, how would you do it?

The conclusion I've come to is: Take control of the content that person consumes.

If you were able to control the TV shows they watch, the movies they saw, the magazines and newspapers they read, the content they consumed on the internet... you could destroy that person's life. A person you've never met. A person you never touched. But by controlling the content of their life, you could destroy them.

And that's exactly what's happening in our society today. People's lives are being destroyed by content. Their lives, their families, their health, their marriages, their psychological equilibrium, and their souls are being decimated by the content they are consuming on a daily basis.

We need to do something about that. We need to prioritize and consume and share content that is helpful and hopeful. We thirst for content that nourishes our souls. We need healthy content diets.

[**Jack**]: That's a really useful analogy. And it brings to mind another great analogy I once read from Padre Pio: "Prayer is oxygen for the soul."

What is the relationship between reclaiming your soul and prayer?

[**Matthew**]: In any of these topics, the first step is working out what has been lost and how it was lost. This is important in order to reclaim what has been lost in a healthy way.

With prayer, we need a deep recognition that we wouldn't have so much to reclaim if we had (a) been taught how to pray at a younger age and (b) sustained a regular, life-giving prayer life consistently throughout our lives. So, it's important we turn the switch on and jump into prayer, that we stop the bleeding in a sense. So that things are not happening today and next week that will need to be reclaimed next year because a new awareness emerges.

The other piece is that prayer provides insight. In some situations where something needs to be reclaimed, we may be so angry about the situation that we can't see past our anger. Prayer and the scriptures give us insight that allow us to be aware of what's happening to us and within us.

Think of one of these situations in your life as a shipwreck. If you go to the shipwreck, you realize the ship is sunk and rotting, but maybe there are only three valuable things on that shipwreck. That's what you really need to reclaim. So, let's scuba dive down to the wreck, get the three valuable things, and get out of here. The ship can stay where it is. You can spend the rest of your life trying to pull the ship up and completely restore it, but other than the three valuable things, it doesn't serve any value.

> *"God speaks in the silence of the heart. Listening is the beginning of prayer."*
>
> - *Mother Teresa*

[Five Ways to Cultivate a Strong Inner Life]

A tree with deep roots can weather any storm. We all experience storms in our lives. It's not a question of *if* but *when* the next storm will come. So begin to prepare today for the coming storms. How? By fostering a rich inner life. Even if your relationship with yourself and with God has been battered in the past, today is a chance to start sinking the deep roots of a strong inner life so you can stand firm in the storms to come and allow your truest self to come into full bloom. Here are 5 ways to begin.

1. **Seek silence and solitude.**

   Who are you? What are you here for? What matters most in your life? What matters least? These are the foundational questions of the inner life. If you want to get clear about the answers, find time for silence and solitude. Our world is noisy, busy and full of distractions. It's in silence and solitude that you will most clearly hear the voice within you and the voice of God in your life.

2. **Spend time with beauty.**

   There are three ancient and powerful forces for enlivening your spirit: truth, beauty, and goodness. Beauty is often neglected or forgotten. We think it is something just for artists, but it's not. Establish a relationship with beauty. Make your home beautiful. Purchase a piece of art that inspires you and hang it. Sit in a beautiful church or in the beauty of nature. Let beauty breathe new life into your soul.

3. **Be intentional with what you consume.**

Jesus says that the "the eye is the lamp of the body." It can flood the soul with either darkness or light. What do you let into your mind, heart, and ultimately your soul through your eyes? That includes what you read, the social media accounts you follow, the television and movies you watch, and so much more. Assess the content you are consuming and start seeking content that feeds your soul with light and goodness.

4. **Guard against evil things that destroy the soul.**

Jesus also says that the greatest threat to our souls comes from within. Anger, jealousy, lust, hatred, unforgiveness, resentment, bitterness—these things corrupt our soul from the inside out. Is it time to cleanse your inner-life of these destructive forces? Reclaiming your soul often begins with the choice to no longer allow these corrosive influences to take up room in your heart, mind, and soul.

5. **Pray.**

Padre Pio once said, "Prayer is oxygen for the soul." That means, in no uncertain terms, that without prayer your soul will die. If you haven't prayed in a while, just take one minute today to pray. Work your way up to praying for 10 minutes a day. This one simple action will transform your life because it will transform the life within you.

You have a soul. You have life within you. It's your choice to either stoke your inner life into a vibrant source of goodness, love, and hope, or allow it to wither into a source of pain, confusion, and destruction. If you want the fruits of goodness, love, and hope, start sinking those deep roots today!

The life that wants to live in you is different than the life you are living.

[priorities]

who and what matters most

[a bit of inspiration]

This is what we long for: unity of life. What is unity of life? It is the sense that our life is one—not many parts or many compartments, but one living, breathing, ordered life. Unity of life gives birth to inner peace. It is the opposite of the conflicted and divided feeling that we are often plagued with. Unity of life is the result of aligning our actions with our beliefs, and it leads to a life of integrity, a life that is whole, a life that is undivided.

Between 1953 and 1981, Peace Pilgrim walked more than twenty-five thousand miles across the United States, spreading her simple message of peace. She talked with people on dusty roads and city streets, to college, church, and civic groups, on TV and radio, discussing peace within and peace in the world. In her writings about inner peace, she spoke of four preparations. The second is of particular interest to us at this time:

"The second preparation has to do with bringing our lives into harmony with the laws that govern this universe. If we are out of harmony through ignorance, we suffer somewhat; but if we know better and are still out of harmony, then we suffer a great deal. I recognized that these laws are well-known and well-believed, and therefore they just needed to be well-lived.

So I got busy on a very interesting project. This was to live all the good things I believed in. I did not confuse myself by trying to take them all at once, but rather, if I was doing something that I knew I should not be doing, I stopped doing it, and I always made a quick relinquishment. You see, that's the easy way. Tapering off is long and hard. And if I was not doing something that I knew I should be doing, I got busy on that. Now if I believe something, I live it. Otherwise, it would be *perfectly meaningless. No life can be in harmony unless belief and practice are in harmony."*

If we ever wish to have harmony in our lives, inner peace, and unity of life, we must begin the work of uniting our actions with our beliefs. In our quest for enduring happiness, it is important that we constantly remind ourselves that happiness is not achieved by the pursuit of happiness but rather is the result of right living. Right living, a life of integrity, is achieved by living through our daily actions all the good things we believe.

[Q & A with Matthew]

[**Jack**]: *Priority was first a singular noun and now it's used in the plural form, so we've adapted the meaning. Any initial reactions to that?*

[**Matthew**]: I do talk about in the plural form as we regularly use it in society. But that is a powerful insight. My immediate reaction is that Jesus uses the singular form. It's not "Seek first the Kingdom of God and also these three other things, and all else will be given to you in addition." It's not "Only three things are necessary." It's "Martha, Martha... only one thing is necessary. And Mary has chosen the better part."

Really powerful insight. I do think we think in terms of priorities, in the plural form. And we do struggle to control the list. We let the list keep getting longer and longer. And of course, if everything is a priority, nothing is a priority.

[**Jack**]: *Do you think that there's a universal order of priority?*

[**Matthew**]: Tough question. Towards the top of the list, yes. As you get into the list, I think it shifts, and I think it can shift for the same person at different times in his or her life. We have different priorities in different seasons in their life. But having any sense of our priorities is going to drive a level of intentionality that most people don't live with.

That intentionality is more important than saying my priorities are right, or my priorities are better than yours, or my priorities are right and yours are wrong.

[**Jack**]: That's interesting. So much of the work is in picking something, because then you can work out whether or not it's the right thing over time. And you can start getting a whole lot closer to where you want to be just by just starting the journey of making intentional choices.

[**Matthew**]: I agree. I think that's a great insight, and very practical. And these types of discussions can easily get theoretical quickly and what people need is practical guidance.

[**Jack**]: Warren Buffett has a quote that says: "The difference between successful people and really successful people is that really successful people say 'no' to almost everything."

What is the relationship between saying 'no' and priorities?

[**Matthew**]: Your 'no' allows you to defend your priorities. Just as your no allows you to defend your character. Just as your no is part of guarding your heart. Being able to say no is an essential life skill.

And again, it's not something that is taught. Oftentimes, the very opposite is taught by all the people who claim to love us, because when we say 'yes' to them, they love us more. So, we get in the habit of saying 'yes' to please them, and then we carry that behavior out into the world and the rest of our lives.

Finding your 'no' is essential.

> *"There is never enough time to do everything, but there is always enough time to do the most important thing."*
>
> *- Brian Tracy*

[**Jack**]: *What do you think some of the fruits are of a rightly-ordered life?*

[**Matthew**]: Peace of mind. Contentment. The sense that you are enough. The belief that you are doing enough.

Most people in modern society do not feel they

are doing enough. And they're right and they're wrong. Because, in most cases they're doing too much. But also, in most cases they're not doing enough of the right things. The most important things are continuously being neglected in favor of the most urgent things.

[**Jack**]: When my wife and I were dating, I was talking with my Dream Manager. He had me do an exercise where I wrote down a physical list of my priorities. I did it, and then asked my wife to tell me, based on the way I was spending my time, what she thought my priorities were. The lists were different in really powerful ways. It was a huge turning point in our relationship and in my life. She was able to mirror back to me a different perception of my priorities. I changed my life because of that conversation. It was eye opening for me to see how little visibility we sometimes have about our own priorities.

What are your thoughts on our own ability to understand where our priorities are and whether or not we're actually living up to them, and ways to grapple with that?

[**Matthew**]: We believe ourselves, which is part of the problem. Our minds are always telling us stuff. And while we believe it to be true, a lot of it isn't true.

Especially when our minds start speculating about what other people are thinking or feeling or why other people arc doing things. Or when we are guessing what motivated another person to do something, you're in a territory where you don't have a chance of getting that right.

But because our mind tells us something, we believe it. And this is a problem in a highly educated society. It's actually a combination of two things: highly educated society and a real lack of humility. People don't question themselves, people don't question their assumptions, people don't explore. Nothing is as it appears to be, including ourselves. And I think that's very important if we're going to get to what you're talking about.

What's most important here is to acknowledge what I will call the gap. Whatever your priorities are, there is always going to be a gap between what they are and how you are living them out each day, week, month, year.

We are deceiving ourselves if we think there is not a gap, and we are deceiving ourselves if we don't think about the gap.

The examination of priorities that your Dream Manager had you do is a powerful exercise. By discussing that with your girlfriend(now wife) you took it a step further and that's an important step, because it forced you out of the wonderland of your mind into the objective reality of life. We should be constantly asking ourselves: What is real? What is imagined? How am I deceiving myself?

But let's look at some practical examples. Suppose someone says, "My priorities are: God, family, friends, work." But then if we look at how that person spends their time and money, we may get a completely different picture. I choose money and time because they provide concrete evidence of what we value.

At the same time, we are in a very gray area. This is far from black and white, which is why it is so easy to deceive ourselves. For example, in the above priority list (#1 God. #2 Family #3 Friends. #4 Work). It's complicated, because #4(work) is part of #2(family), by working hard we support our families. And #4(work) is a way of loving God(#1), but if that is the only way we commune with God it will be insufficient. Just as if the only way we fulfill our prioritization of family is by working then we have strayed from our priorities, or are deceiving ourselves, or both.

> *"If you chase two rabbits, you will not catch either one."*
>
> - *Russian Proverb*

[Jack]: *You've said a lot of times "Our lives change when our habits change." How does that relate to our priorities?*

[Matthew]: We're in the territory of talking about the ordered life, the ethical life, the moral life, the disciplined life. Think about it this way: the person who gets up and goes running at 5:30 every morning often doesn't even think about it, it's just part of who they are. They don't toss and turn in bed for 30 minutes thinking about whether or not they'll do it, or what they could do instead, or whatever else. They just do it. It is an ingrained habit, an unquestioned part of their day.

The same applies to patience, honesty, courage, empathy, compassion, kindness, generosity. As you build these things, they stand when you're in the mood for it, and when you're not in the mood for it. The problem is, when we lack priorities (or a philosophy) and we need to make a choice, we need to build a philosophy from the ground up. Like you've got this one choice to make, but now you have to decide on a whole worldview, build a philosophy, and discern your priorities—just to make a single choice or decision.

You mentioned earlier that as an exercise, you made a list of your priorities. How long did it take you?

[**Jack**]: Not that long. Maybe 15 or 20 minutes.

[**Matthew**]: Okay, great. It didn't seem like long, because you weren't under pressure to make a decision. But now, imagine if every time you had to make a decision, you needed to establish your priorities first. You'd be completely paralyzed. That's what happens to people in an unordered life, with no philosophy, no worldview. They stop thinking about the decision and just do what they feel like doing, because it is just too overwhelming. They don't live lives of considered action, it's unconsidered action. The unconsidered life is made up of a lot of unconsidered choices and actions.

Investing the upfront time to establish our priorities is time well-spent. Taking time to revisit our priorities to ensure our lives align with our priorities is time very well spent. It saves us from hundreds of hours of inner turmoil.

It is also essential that we refrain from judging people who are not clear about their priorities. One reason is because most people are never blessed to be taken through an exercise like your Dream Manager walked you through. Never in their whole lives. And so, we return to a familiar theme, so many of the lessons that are essential to living with passion and purpose, so much of what we need to know in order to flourish as human beings we are not taught at any time in life.

There is something else I find it is important to be present to. The world is a very scary place for people who don't have a life philosophy. Life is hard enough and can certainly be scary at times even if you do have a clear sense of what matters most and what matters least. So, if we have some clarity around these things, I think we have three responsibilities: to be grateful; to have compassion for those that do not; and, to help as many people as possible develop in these areas.

"Things which matter most must never be at the mercy of things which matter least."

- Johann Wolfgang von Goethe

[Five Ways to Set Priorities]

When was the last time you said, "I don't have time!" either to an idea in your mind, one of your passions, or a person? What was it that you didn't have time to do? For most people it's something like spending time with family and friends, exercising, or preparing a healthy meal. For all of us at one time or another it is prayer. There will always be things we don't have time for. The key is making sure those aren't the most important things in our lives. That starts with getting crystal clear about our priorities. Here's five ways to carve out more time and energy for the things that matter most.

1. **Consider four fundamental questions.**
   Who are you? What are you here for? What matters most? What matters least? The clearer you become about the answers to these four questions, the clearer your true priorities will

become. Most people don't get clear about these questions, and that means they are stumbling around half-blind when trying to live an ordered and meaningful life. Sit with these questions for a few minutes often.

2. **Don't just reflect. Write!**

Write your priorities down. Putting them on paper moves them from the realm of "I think these are my priorities" into a concrete list that you can use to hold yourself accountable. It isn't quite setting them in stone, but it is a simple action that forces you to get clear about your priorities and give them greater weight in your life.

3. **Dream.**

Dream about who you might become and what you might do if you lived your priorities. How would your life change if you dedicated your time and energy to the most important things in your life? What would you have to stop doing? How would you feel if you were consistently living in accord with your priorities? Asking yourself questions like these can generate the energy and enthusiasm you need to make your priorities a reality in your life.

4. **Check your schedule (and bank account) against your priorities.**

None of us sticks to our priorities 100%. All of us are at least partially deluded about how much we are currently aligned with what we say are our priorities. Compare your written list of priorities to your schedule. Does how you spend your time line up with what you say your priorities are? If not, start scheduling in your priorities to make sure you honor them. (Also consider evaluating what you spend money on—this tells us a lot about what we really value too).

5. **Practice saying 'no' to things that infringe on your priorities.**

Once you establish your priorities clearly, everything else you could do with your time, money and energy becomes a distraction or temptation not to follow them. Your greatest tool for defending and protecting your priorities is your ability to say no. Practice saying no to the less important things that vie for your time and attention. In the long run, this will earn you more respect and solidify your priorities.

It is a great skill in life to decide what is really important and necessary, make it a priority, and do what matters most. Without this skill, the siren call of a world full of shinny things will always keep us busy and distracted from what really counts. It is difficult, yes, but if you dedicate yourself to assessing your priorities and reallocating your time and energy to those things, you will become a person fully alive, striving to grow, becoming ever more who you were meant to be.

The life that wants to live in you is different than the life you are living.

[money and things]

financial assets and tangible material possessions

[a bit of inspiration]

Once upon a time there was a boy who was growing up in a very wealthy family. One day, his father decided to take him on a trip to show him how other people who were less fortunate lived. His father's goal was to help his son appreciate everything that he has been given in life.

The boy and his father pulled up to a farm where a very poor family lived. They spent several days on the farm, helping the family work for their food and take care of their land.

When they left the farm, the dad asked his son if he enjoyed their trip and if he had learned anything during the time they spent with this other family.

The boy quickly replied, "It was fantastic, that family is so lucky!"

Confused, his father asked what he meant by that.

The boy said, "Well, we only have one dog, but that family has four—and they have chickens! We have four people in our home, but they have 12! They have so many people to play with! We have a pool in our yard, but they have a river running through their property that is endless. We have lanterns outside so we can see at night, but they have the wide open sky and the beautiful stars to give them wonder and light. We have a patio, but they have the entire horizon to enjoy—they have endless fields to run around in and play. We have to go to the grocery store, but they are able to grow their own food. Our high fence protects our property and our family, but they don't need such a limiting structure, because their friends protect them."

The father was speechless.

Finally, the boy added, "Thank you for showing me how rich people live, they're so lucky."

[Q & A with Matthew]

[**Jack**]: Alright, let's talk about money and things. Jesus said, "It is easier for a camel to pass through the eye of a needle than a rich person to go to heaven."

Does that mean that money and things are evil?

[**Matthew**]: No, but it should give us pause in a number of ways. First, we are quick to dismiss this thinking that we are not rich, and that is a mistake. Most of the people reading this are richer than the richest people of say the 12th century from a purely "things of this world" perspective. But the second thing we need to careful with here is how we define rich. We tend to define it narrowly, isolating it to financial assets and tangible material possessions. That is a mistake that reveals something about the content of our hearts.

Money isn't the source of all evil, love of money is the problem. Money itself is neutral, it's what we do with it or don't do with it that gives money it's positive or negative charge.

[Jack]: *Why do you think Jesus talks about money more than any other topic?*

[Matthew]: I think because it is potentially the most significant obstacle to our spiritual growth. In *The Four Signs of a Dynamic Catholic*, I note how through a conversation with friends, I realized that if you are not generous with your money, you are unlikely to be generous with your heart. I wrote, "To help people grow spiritually, we need to help them develop a healthy relationship with money." I believe that and I believe we also need to provide people with a holistic approach to money. The conversation about the spirituality of money tends to be confined to giving. This needs to be expanded, built out, to help people develop a spiritual approach to earning money, saving money, spending money, and investing money. Without this holistic approach our spiritual approach to giving will always be incomplete.

The reason why Jesus talks about money more than any other topic is because we erroneously begin to believe that money removes us from the need for God's Providence. It makes us think we don't need God to provide for us. We stop thinking about God's Providence.

It's also important to remember that this is a particularly modern phenomenon. We did not have wealth in ages past like you have wealth today, primarily because you couldn't store wealth prior to the introduction of currency. Around the time of Francis is when currency became widely used and popular. This is why Francis dealt with so many of the problems that mirror in some ways what we deal with today. People for the first time were able to store wealth.

Prior to that you didn't put 10 years worth of

grain in the barn, because you knew it would rot or rodents would come and eat it. You could have 500 sheep, but you couldn't have 10 million sheep. And so, our ability to store wealth makes us think that our needs are taken care of for a certain period of time. But it isn't so.

Financial planners often talk about how you should have three months' worth of cash stored as your emergency fund. If you've got enough money for a year, you may think you don't need anything for the next year. But it isn't so.

In God we live and move and have our being. If you think you don't need anything for the next second, you are wrong. Our need for God's providence is continuous and unending.

Money has a way of disconnecting us from our real needs. Above all else, human beings need. We need many, many things, but first we need God, in him we live and move and breathe, and that is not going to change.

These are some of the ways money becomes a

spiritual obstacle because we forget how much and how constantly we need God.

> *"Act as if everything depended on you; trust as if everything depended on God."*
> - St. Ignatius of Loyola

[**Jack**]: *Fulton Sheen famously said: "You must remember to love people and use things." What do you think about that quote?*

[**Matthew**]: The more material a society becomes, the more secular a society becomes. Our whole worldview comes from an understanding of the human person. Our thoughts around any issue can be traced back to our vision of the human person.

All problems in the world today can be traced back to an erroneous or distorted view of what it means to be a human being.

As Christians, our vision of the human person is that the human person is infinitely valuable in and of himself or herself. Not because of anything he or she does or has, but simply by the fact that he or she has been created purposefully by God. Each person is a child of God. A lot of dignity and esteem come from that fact alone. But materialism, secularism, and the godlessness of our age robs people of all that dignity and esteem.

As the world becomes more materialistic and more secular people do become just pawns in other people's chess games. We do use people. People are being used increasingly. I don't think anyone can look at the world and say otherwise.

[**Jack**]: Honestly, the first time I thought about the idea of reclaiming money and things, I thought about my son. He's at that age where, when he gets a new toy, his instinct is to call it "mine."

Does reclaiming money and things mean making them "mine" again?

[**Matthew**]: The opposite actually. Reclaiming money and things means reclaiming *a right relationship* with money and things. That right relationship consists primarily of understanding that nothing is ours, all is gift, we are stewards of the gifts entrusted to us. And there are good stewards and bad stewards, and some days I am a good steward and some days I am a bad steward of all that has been entrusted to me. I suspect the same is true for us all if we examine ourselves. The important thing is that we continue to strive for a right relationship with the things of this world and to be good stewards.

[**Jack**]: Understood. That said, *how do you reclaim a right relationship with money and things?*

[**Matthew**]: You reclaim a right relationship with money by realizing that none of it actually belongs to you, that you're a steward of it, and that you're responsible for how you deal with it. We are in an age that wants to speak only of rights, but all rights come with responsibilities.

You also reclaim a right relationship with things by ensuring that you can live without them. By developing appropriate detachment from money and things we are able to allow them to have their rightful place on our list of priorities. By being able to say, "This car is nice, but I can live without it," and knowing that to be true, that we give things their right place in our lives.

Interestingly, by placing things in their rightful place, we are able to enjoy them most. And it is important to recognize that part of that right relationship is the wisdom that some things bring you incredible joy even though they are just things, and there's nothing wrong with that.

"If a man is proud of his wealth, he should not be praised until it is known how he employs it."

- *Socrates*

[**Jack**]: I knew this great priest, who I haven't talked to in a long time. When he was a seminarian, he got a scholarship to go live and study in Jerusalem where he basically owned nothing. His family had a third car that they let him use when he was on assignment in the States for the summer. It was a BMW. And it caused a huge uproar in his parish. People thought it was inappropriate that he had this nice car. Little did they know the car had been loaned to him.

How does our relationship with money and things affect the way we view other people's money and things?

[**Matthew**]: I want to focus in on one thing you said: "People thought it was inappropriate that he had this nice car." I want to further focus in on two words: "He had."

He had the car, but that doesn't mean the car had him. In fact, it is distinctly possible that his critics were more affected by the car than the seminarian was.

There is a story about two monks on pilgrimage when they come to a river. There's a beautiful young woman who's trying to cross the river. One of the monks just picks her up in his arms and carries her across the river. He does it as if without thought and as if it were the most natural thing in the world. On the other side, he sets her down and the monks and the woman head off in different directions to continue their journeys. As the two monks continue walking together, the other monk fell into a resentful silence for hours.

Finally, the monk who carried the woman across the river says, "Brother, what's troubling your mind?" The other monk replies, "It was completely inappropriate for you to touch that woman." The monk who carried the woman across the river smiled and said, "I carried her across the river, but it seems you are still carrying her."

That's what it's about. I've met many people over the past thirty years who have considerable wealth. The majority of them are not as attached to their money and things as people assume.

When people saw that seminarian with a BMW, they projected their own distorted relationship with money and things onto him. It doesn't say something about the seminarian. It says something about those who judged him.

"Man should not consider his material possession his own, but as common to all, so as to share them without hesitation when others are in need."
- *Thomas Aquinas*

[Five Ways to Improve Your Relationship with Money and Things]

You have a God-sized hole. The world is constantly trying to seduce you into believing that if you just got enough money and things, you could fill that hole. But nothing on this earth can fill the hole. Only God can liberate you from your emptiness. Does that mean money and things are nothing more than evil distractions? No. In fact, while money and things can be a stumbling block, they can also be a powerful means of strengthening our relationship with God and becoming better-versions-of-ourselves. Here are five ways to establish a healthy relationship with money and things.

1. Treat money like a tool.

Money is a neutral entity. It isn't inherently good or bad. Having it doesn't make you a better person or increase your worth, nor does not having it. And so, the first step to a right relationship with money is acknowledging the current role it plays in your life. If you've attached any part of your sense of self to money, remind yourself that money is just a tool. It's a powerful tool you can use to serve others, bring enjoyment to your life, foster stability for your future, and more. But it's still just a tool.

2. **Pay yourself.**

This is one of the golden rules of financial planning, it is also common sense, and it also fulfills a responsibility we have to ourselves and others we are responsible for supporting. With every paycheck, save a set amount of money. Put it aside in a separate savings or retirement account. Some people call this a "rainy day" fund. What they mean is: unexpected things are always happening in life. People get sick or injured, important things break, emergencies happen. Putting aside money each paycheck creates a healthy attitude toward money as a tool and helps you develop long-term vision.

3. **Create non-negotiables.**

   It's easy for money and things to define our relationship with them if we don't do the work of defining the relationship for ourselves. Create and follow some simple rules for yourself when it comes to money. For example: Don't spend more than you make; don't take on debt carelessly or unnecessarily; try to give more to those in need this year than last year. They may seem basic, but making some simple rules non-negotiable in your relationship with money will take some bad outcomes off the table before they ever even come up.

4. **Know the difference between needs and wants.**

   You want to go to the concert, but you need to buy food. We know there is a difference between needs and wants, but this distinction can have an enormous impact on our relationship with money and things if we are not clear. It doesn't help that our advertising drenched culture wants to convince you that what you want is what you actually need. Whenever you are making a purchase, first get clear on one question: is this a need or a want? That doesn't mean you only buy what you need, but it puts what you want in proper perspective.

5. **Buy things that bring you joy.**

This is where so many people get tripped up or lose heart before they ever start reshaping their relationship with money and things. They mistakenly believe a good relationship with money and things means giving away all of your money and having no "unnecessary" things. We don't need to be ashamed of buying things that bring us joy. God has made that desire and joy possible for a reason. He wants us to experience desire and joy, and he wants us to recognize that there is a limit to the joy the things of this world can bring us. And he wants us to keep following those desires and that joy, because he knows it will lead us ultimately to what we desire more than anything else (God) and what will bring us unending joy (eternity with God). So, whether it's an expensive cup of coffee, a new pair of shoes, new golf clubs, a nice car... allow these things to bring you great joy, just remember that all the things in this world will not satisfy you because what you desire ultimately is to taste the good things of the next world.

Money and things are a crucial aspect of life. Our relationship with them determines our approach to the world and our capacity for fulfillment. We can allow them to drag us to a place of greed, discontent, identity confusion, and mistaken priorities. Or we direct the relationship and harness these things as tools to bring purpose, generosity, and joy into our lives and the lives of others.

The life that wants to live in you is different than the life you are living.

[hope for the future]

confidence that good and beautiful things
will happen in the future

[a bit of inspiration]

It was Paul's time. He could see it in the doctor's eyes.
After ninety-two years of life, Paul was ready to go back
to God. His last request was to spend a private moment
with each special person gathered around his bed.

Three children, five grandchildren, a coworker, and
two lifelong friends shared the final hours of Paul's life.
Words of love, appreciation, and forgiveness. Tears of
sorrow. Tears of laughter. Each person left the room
feeling lighter than they had in years. Peace came with
each encounter. A peace that only comes from spending
time with a life well lived.

Outside in the waiting area, nervous and a bit scared, Connor waited for his turn. Connor was Paul's grandson. When Connor was ten, his dad left him, his mother, and his two younger brothers. Connor's mom, Paul's daughter, wanted her three sons to have a strong role model, so she moved the family into her father's house. A recent widower, Paul was thankful for the company.

In the early years, Paul taught Connor everything he knew: how to fish, how to live as a man of integrity, and how to pray. In the later years, the roles changed. As Paul's body began to fail him, Connor took his grandfather to Mass on Sunday; he helped him get dressed in the morning and ready for bed at night; and he stayed up late listening to old Frank Sinatra records when Paul was in too much pain to sleep. The two men loved each other on a level words could not express.

Connor wasn't yet ready to say good-bye. Paul was his rock, his role model, and his best friend. Connor wondered how he would navigate life without him. Connor was the last one to visit his grandfather. He walked in and sat down next to Paul, who had his eyes closed. When he opened his eyes, Paul smiled at his grandson. Immediately Connor began to weep. "I don't want to lose you!" he shouted and buried his head in his grandfather's chest.

Paul took a deep breath and savored the moment. He remembered the day Connor was born, how he had fit in the palm of his hand. Paul thanked God for sending him such a friend so late in life. Paul lifted his grandson's chin so they could look each other in the eye.

"Son, we'll always be together, you know that. Just pray for me on this side of heaven and know I'll be praying for you on the other. Then one day we'll meet again." He wiped the tears from his grandson's eyes; they shared a smile, and hugged one last time.

[Q & A with Matthew]

[Jack]: *How can you identify a person of hope?*

[**Matthew**]: Hope lives in our hearts, but it also lives in our words and actions. Hope resides in our choices. Hope resides in how we choose to spend our lives to.

The evidence of hope manifests in a person's life in an endless number of ways, large and small. Take for example something as ordinary as saving money. Saving money is an act of hope. If you had no confidence in the future, you wouldn't save money. The opposite is also true, those who are able to save but do not save, are saying in some small way, "I have no hope in the future."

The other thing to keep in mind here is that hope is not permanent. You may be full of hope today, but you might not be a person of hope tomorrow.

This is true for me every day. Hope is something that has to be received and won and fought for and defended every day. You cannot depend on your past. It certainly is helpful, but you have to strive to be a person of hope every day. You have to decide to be a person of hope every day.

And part of that means paying attention to the

people, things, and experiences that increase your hope, and those that try to steal it.

[**Jack**]: Let's use the wisdom of opposites here.

What does despair teach us about hope?

[**Matthew**]: Okay so, this is a half-baked thought that I've been working on, but I think despair is the result of a particularly selfish way of looking at things. When we're in despair, we tend to be inward focused. We're not saying it's the end of the world, we're saying my reality is being crushed, or something that's important to me has been taken from me. Interestingly, despair is also short-sighted. It's like we are trapped in the now and ignore the future as it doesn't exist.

In order to maintain hope, we have to take the long view. How hopeful are you for the Church in the next 48 hours? Not that hopeful. We have a lot of problems that are going to take some time to correct and improve. How hopeful are you for the Church in the next thousand years? The timeframe changes everything.

Think about people who are in a relationship they think is hopeless. They are likely thinking about now, or today, or last week, or the next two weeks. They are probably not thinking about the next 10 or 20 years and the problems they may encounter amidst all the wonderful that will happen over the next decade or two.

"Control your own destiny or someone else will."
- Jack Welch

[**Jack**]: *Can you have a victim mentality and still be hopeful?*

[**Matthew**]: Probably not. But you can be a victim and be hopeful. There is a difference between being a victim of something or someone and having a victim mentality. Many of the people who have suffered most horrifically in history do not think of themselves as victims. I think it's beautiful that we refer to those who survived the Holocaust as survivors, not victims.

I think of Viktor Frankl's work on logotherapy after his experiences in the concentration camps, where he was focused on the idea that meaning can trump extreme suffering and horrific circumstances. I think this provides some of the greatest evidence of modern times that hope can survive. Whatever it is we are going through, hope can survive.

You find a lot of hopeful people in some of the darkest moments in history. This puts how easily I become discouraged some days in perspective.

[Jack]: *What is the relationship between the past and hope?*

[Matthew]: Any relationship is multifaceted and that is true here.

One aspect is that by recognizing how God has moved in our life in the past, provided for us in the past, given to us even when we thought he was taking from us at the time, we develop the hope and belief that God will move in our lives in the future. Not perhaps always as we wish, but with the whole picture in mind.

Another is by drawing on a longer view of history and recognizing that whatever our circumstances may be, many, many people have been in worse circumstances and have prevailed over those circumstances. So, I think that we can draw hope from the example of people in the past.

On a more personal level, looking back in our own lives allows us to reflect on what we have overcome in the past with God's help, much of which we may have thought was insurmountable at the time. That can serve as a source of strength of hope for the future. I do think the past serves very powerfully in providing hope for the future.

> *"Change is the law of life. And those who look only to the past or present are certain to miss the future."*
> – *John F. Kennedy*

[**Jack**]: What is the relationship between being a person of possibility and hope?

[**Matthew**]: A person of possibilities believes the future can be bigger than the past and that he or she can do something to bring that bigger, better, more beautiful future about. These are just intrinsically hopeful positions.

We all deal with disappointments in life. It's important to examine them. Was the disappointment the result of someone else's thoughtless or malicious behavior? Was it the result of unreasonable or unrealistic expectations? Unrealistic expectations can create false hope that is sure to be crushed eventually. So, it's important to examine our hopes and expectations to ensure we have not wandered beyond hope and optimism into a place where we have become disconnected from reality.

"What is coming is better than what is gone."
- *Arabic Proverb*

[**Jack**]: What gives you hope?

[**Matthew**]: The first thing I want to note is that my hope is attacked on a regular basis, and at times viciously attacked. The things I spend my life thinking about and reading about, my interactions with people, tend to be focused on some of the most serious things people are experiencing and can therefore drain you of hope.

I remember when I used to read and reply to all my emails. At the end of each day I would be just exhausted, emotionally exhausted. The intimate and heart-breaking things that people share with you over an email, and the pain and suffering that people are carrying around inside them every day is astounding. To do this work, your hope is going to be brutally attacked regularly, and I think it's important to be mindful of that.

The other thing is that I am not a hopeful person every day of the week, and I think it's important people around me understand that, that the reader understands that, and that I understand that.

What brings me hope? My capacity to change. The astounding changes I've seen other people make in their lives, in their relationships, in their organizations, in their communities. Our humanity, my humanity and your humanity. When humans are at their best it is so beautiful. And life itself. Life brings me hope.

There are many threats to human hope, primarily violence and poverty. Violence and poverty have a way eradicating hope. But I believe human beings who are unthreatened by poverty and violence wish good things for their neighbors. I believe we want to live in each other's happiness, not misery. And I believe that most people will do what they can to bring about good things for each other. That gives me hope.

I also draw hope from our capacity for goodness. I've just seen so many people who want to do good, so much good, and that brings me hope.

[Five Ways to Infuse Your Life with Hope]

It's never too late for a new beginning. It's never too late to start over again. It's never too late to choose to become the-best-version-of-yourself. No matter where we are in life, God is inviting us in some way to be a person of possibility, a person who never gives up on the possibility that our future can be bigger and brighter and more beautiful than our past. Here are five short and simple ways to invite hope and possibility back into your life.

1. Cheer for yourself.

The most powerful way to start a habit is not repetition. It's actually through a deep emotional connection. You can't have hope for the future if you don't feel good about yourself. Next time you choose the-best-version-of-yourself over some lesser-version-of-yourself, celebrate that. Literally yell out a cheer for yourself. Loudly. Your body will respond in kind, filling you with hope that things can get better.

2. **Reflect on past wins.**

Take 10 minutes out of your day, grab some paper, and describe an experience where something you hoped for became a reality. It's been proven again and again that merely reliving a positive experience from the past has the power to rewrite the script in your mind about your current situation with a narrative of hope.

3. **Be creative.**

Did you know that people of hope tend to be more creative? It's true. Hope opens us up to different ideas and different ways of solving the problems before us. The reverse is also true. If you are looking for hope, start doing something that expands your creativity and helps you to see the amazing possibilities that you struggled to see previously.

4. **Pray.**

Science has started to confirm what spiritual

giants have known for centuries: prayer de-
creases stress, depression, and blood-pressure,
and increases self-esteem. It leads to improved
health and strengthens relationships. And
prayer, emotionally and spiritually, increases
hope.

5. **Keep an inspiration journal.**
Get yourself a notebook and start filling it with
things that inspire you, move your heart, and
stir your soul. You can write dreams you want
to accomplish or hopes for the future. You can
fill it with quotes or images that give you courage and energy for life. It can be whatever you
want it to be so long as it inspires you. On days
when you feel a little lost or doubtful about the
future, pick up your inspiration journal and
start flipping through it. It will show you things
that once seemed impossible that became true.
It will show you how the things you thought
were so important once aren't so important
now. It will show you the road back to hope.

If we are to become the people God dreams of us becoming, we need hope. Some people say that hope only sets you up for disappointment, and because of that hope is a bad thing. Hope is a good thing, maybe the best of things. Hope is one of those things that you can't buy, but that will be freely given to you if you ask. Hope is the one thing people cannot live without, and something nobody can take from you.

I hope... I hope I can live up to the gifts and talents God has given me. I hope I can have the courage to be a true friend, a good father, and a loving husband. I hope I never stop striving to become the-best-version-of-myself. I hope I will continue to take time to listen to the voice of God each day. I hope I will have the courage to follow where his voice leads me. I hope we can build a world where our children can grow free and strong. I hope . . . and that is a wonderful thing. Join me in that hope and together we will awaken all men and women to discover the incredible dream God has for their lives and for the world.

How can you find and bring hope to others today?

The life that wants to live in you is different than the life you are living.

[acknowledgments]

Writing is a solitary calling. It consists of thousands of hours alone in the quiet of my study. For thirty years, I have dedicated myself to this craft, trying each day to improve, so that I can find the right combination of words to most beautifully share the ideas that fill my heart. Writing has been the source of immense satisfaction and glorious frustration. I wouldn't trade any of it. But this project was different. I worked on it with a team and what a pleasure it has been.

First and foremost, I would like to thank Jack Beers for his vison and leadership, for seeking to understand why I write, what I have written, what the craft of writing means to me, and why I write the way I do.

Next, Stephen Anderson, Ashley Dias, and Mary Joy Kozak for pouring their time, energy, and talent into the project and bringing this work to life.

I would also like to thank: Evan Atkins; Katie Beers; Claire Darnell; Meg Berberich, and Hannah Hubert for their contributions and support.

Together as a team you have done something special here. It will touch many lives I am confident of that. But it will also change you forever, and one Sunday afternoon many years from now, you will look back upon the summer of 2021, smile upon these days, and know that they changed you forever. On that day, please know, that wherever I am, I am grateful that we had this experience together.

Matthew Kelly

[about the author]

matthew kelly is a best-selling author, speaker, thought leader, entrepreneur, consultant, spiritual leader, and innovator.

He has dedicated his life to helping people and organizations become the-best-version-of-themselves. Born in Sydney, Australia, he began speaking and writing in his late teens while he was attending business school. Since that time, 5 million people have attended his seminars and presentations in more than 50 countries.

Today, Kelly is an internationally acclaimed speaker, author, and business consultant. His books have been published in more than 30 languages, have appeared on the *New York Times*, *Wall Street Journal*, and *USA Today* bestseller lists, and have sold more than 45 million copies.

In his early-twenties he developed "the-best-version-of-yourself" concept and has been sharing it in every arena of life for more than twenty-five years. It is quoted by presidents and celebrities, athletes and their coaches, business leaders and innovators, though perhaps it is never more powerfully quoted than when a mother or father asks a child, "Will that help you become the-best-version-of-yourself?"

Kelly's personal interests include golf, music, art, literature, investing, spirituality, and spending time with his wife, Meggie, and their children Walter, Isabel, Harry, Ralph, and Simon.

[also by matthew kelly]

Life Is Messy

The Rhythm of Life

The Seven Levels of Intimacy

Perfectly Yourself

Resisting Happiness

Amazing Possibilities

I Heard God Laugh

Dig the Well Before You Get Thirsty

Building Better Families

Rediscover Jesus

The Dream Manager

The Culture Solution

Off Balance

The Long View